Praise for James Woodford and *The Secret Life of Wombats*

'Woodford has done the research, he has read widely, spoken with the major wombat pundits and with the lay observers. He has travelled to gain direct experience of all species. His book has drawn together much of what is known about wombats...I know more about wombats than I did, and retain some stark images which I hope never to lose.'
Sunday Age

'To the extent that he has set out to collect and make readable everything the lay reader ought to know about these burly sprinters the book is a great success.'
Canberra Times

'A revealing look at our most personable marsupials.'
Sunday Mail

'Full of endlessly diverting information about wombats...Who would have thought that wombats had a secret life, let alone it being so interesting? And if you think the wombats are interesting you should read about the people who study them!'
Australian Bookseller & Publisher

'Outstandi
Tim Fisch

GW00537806

THE SECRET LIFE OF WOMBATS

James Woodford was born in New South Wales in 1968, and is a science and environment writer for the *Sydney Morning Herald*. In his early twenties he won an *Australian Geographic* Young Adventurer of the Year Award. In 1996 he won the Eureka Prize for environmental journalism and he was awarded the prestigious Michael Daley Prize for science journalism in 1996 and 1997. He is the author of the critically acclaimed bestseller *The Wollemi Pine*. He lives in Sydney.

JAMES WOODFORD

THE SECRET LIFE OF WOMBATS

TEXT PUBLISHING

MELBOURNE AUSTRALIA

ILLUSTRATIONS

Grateful acknowledgment is made to the following for permission to reproduce illustrative material used in the picture section and text: Christo Baars, p. 198; Ron Dibben, p. 180; Brendan Esposito, p. 74, p. 79; John Field, p. 167; Peter Nicholson, plates X, XI, XII, XIII, p. 5, p. 22, p. 32; Kevin O'Daly, p. 176; Peter Schouten, commissioned drawings, p. 84, p. 85, p. 112, p. 143, p. 183; Garry K. Smith, plate VII; Rick Stevens, plates III & VI, p. 48; Dave Watts, plate V; State Library of Victoria, plates I & II, p. 45; all other photographs taken by the author.

The Text Publishing Company
171 La Trobe Street
Melbourne Victoria 3000
Australia

First published 2001, reprinted 2001

Printed and bound by Griffin Press
Designed by Chong Weng-ho
Typeset in 13.3/19 Centaur by J&M Typesetting
Map on x-xi by Tony Fankhauser

National Library of Australia
Cataloguing-in-Publication data:

Woodford, James, 1968– .
The secret life of wombats.
Bibliography.
Includes index.
ISBN 1 876485 86 8.
1. Wombats. 2. Wombats - Habitat. 3. Wombats - Evolution.
I. Title.
599.24

This project has been assisted by the Commonwealth Government through the Australia Council, its arts funding and advisory body.

For Prue
and her love of nature

Never climb down into wombat burrows. They are unstable and full of poisonous animals such as snakes and spiders. Wild dogs use the tunnels as hiding places and wombats themselves are dangerous animals when cornered—easily able to crush intruders against the roof of their homes.

CONTENTS

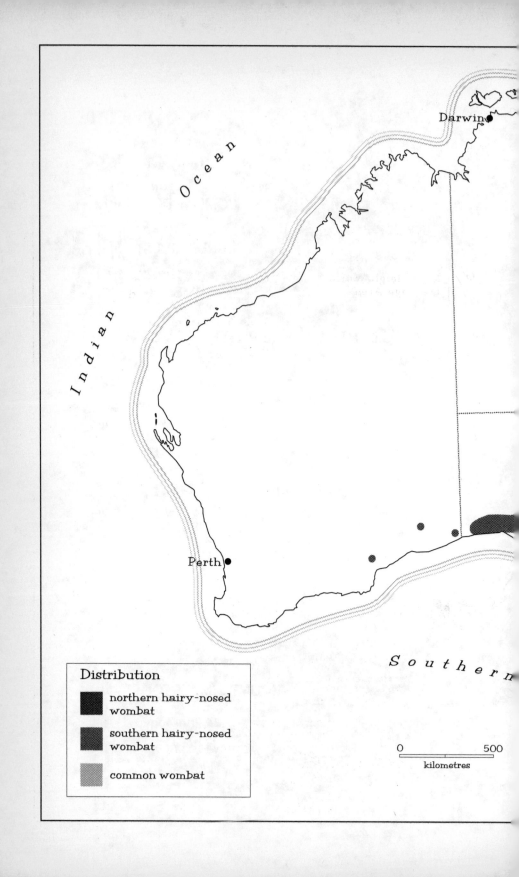

O c e a n

Indian

Darwin

Perth

S o u t h e r n

Distribution

■ northern hairy-nosed
wombat

■ southern hairy-nosed
wombat

common wombat

0   500
kilometres

Chapter 1
WOMBAT BOY

The wombat is a buff to greyish-black, coarse-haired, thick-set animal about three feet long, and it stands only about one foot three inches high. It is heavy (often about 70 pounds in weight) and its weight is carried by its short, thick legs. It is very strong and when seen in a hurry looks like a tank as it takes all types of hills and gullies in its stride. It leaves a footprint like a foreshortened human footprint in mud or snow.

PETER NICHOLSON

By the time he reached the end of the burrow, the ball of twine that trailed behind fifteen-year-old Peter John Nicholson had shrunk from the size of a tennis ball down to that of an apple core. It was April 1960, a few months into the school year at Timbertop—one of the most spartan schools in Australia. Only small signs indicate its location; a rough dirt road is the only way in. The Timbertop campus lies hidden at the base of the mountain. Just a few steps away from the grounds and a student could be lost for days.

Nicholson—PJ or Peter John to his friends and many of his teachers—was playing truant from his dormitory. If caught he may have copped a caning, so he waited until after dark when he could hear that his fellow boarders were fast asleep. He dressed quietly, putting on rubber-soled hiking boots, an old long-sleeved khaki shirt and a tatty football jumper with padding on its elbows. His 'wombatting' pants had patches on patches, so much so that he looked like a boy who had put on every pair of trousers he owned. At the exit to the dormitory he looked out into the night, checking for the red glow of a cigarette or any other sign of a master on the prowl for stray students. Teacher patrols, however, were mainly to prevent inter-dormitory raids and pranks. As long as Nicholson was on his own and keeping quiet, he was able to slip away easily, sneaking across the few illuminated metres between his building and the immense forest.

Another twenty metres and he was on the banks of Timbertop Creek, which he could jump, with one big bound. The waterway supplied the school and it was rich with platypuses and yabbies—a gurgling, crystal-clear stream with deep cold pools. Wombats lived all along its banks and had made useful trails for the exploring boy. He could disappear in seconds by walking up that creek, and from there he could access hundreds of square kilometres of virgin wilderness.

It was now about 9.30 p.m. It was very cold and he braced himself inside his wombatting clothes. Once on the other side of the stream he was free and alone with the forest's nocturnals. His torch caught the red eyes of greater gliders—flying marsupials, with charcoal fur and long agile tails—on the boughs of the mountain-ash eucalypts. Weighing over one and a half kilograms and at over a metre in length, these marsupials spread the membrane of loose skin attached from their elbows to their ankles and can glide up to a hundred metres from tree to tree.

Grey kangaroos turned towards Nicholson but continued grazing as he strode past them. Feral dogs, cats and foxes had not yet penetrated the wilderness and the vegetation was dense with marsupials. There were no weeds, no rubbish, no pollution. The area teemed with wildlife, even in the middle of the day. From the moment he'd arrived at the school in February, Nicholson had noticed and marvelled at the native animals. By the end of his first month he had already investigated more than twenty kilometres from his dormitory. When he and his friends stood outside their dorms for rollcall they could see the kangaroos boxing in the grassy areas beneath the giant trees. Kangaroos may have doe-like faces but during these matches they used their tails like the third leg of a tripod and were capable of tearing at each other's chests until they were stained pink with blood. But it was the wombats which captivated him and lured him outside at night. His destination as he sneaked out of his bed was underground.

In the last month he had been casing one burrow in particular, getting to know its forks and offshoots, testing it for its stability, mapping it and slowly pushing further inside. He had been underground, fashioning turning points and widening routes in places where the tunnel became too narrow for him to pass. He avoided any major excavations though, mindful that the burrow had an occupant.

The boy, already 183 centimetres (six feet) tall and skinny, estimated from the twine still bundled in his hand that he was about ten metres underground. He felt compelled to keep wriggling forward; he couldn't resist exploring deeper and deeper. This was not the first time he had entered a wombat burrow, but this was the furthest he had yet travelled

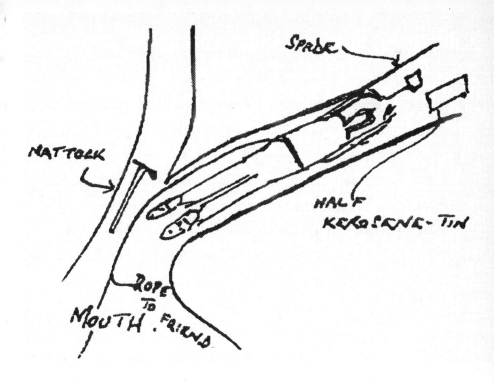

The long and lean Nicholson was a tight fit in a burrow, as shown here in his drawing of how he explored wombat homes.

and he knew that he must be near whatever was living inside. He was entering the foundations of Mount Timbertop. His arms were thrust out in front of him and only a few centimetres lay between his back and the roof of the tunnel. He resembled a caterpillar in its cocoon and he was moving like one, dirt and grit gluing to him as he pushed forward.

It smelt earthy—not bad at all, only a slight waft of vegetation. He was constantly surprised how clean the burrows were. Wombats, he had found, smell like the bush—

they certainly didn't defecate underground. The occasional fibrous root swung in his path and Nicholson thought about the forest that was growing above his head. Thousands of tonnes of timber were separated from him by a ceiling of dirt just a few metres thick.

For a few seconds he turned off his torch and smiled to himself at the complete darkness he was travelling through. Without a light, the air was so black it was a sensation instead of a colour. He even imagined that he could see the electric messages firing around in his brain. It was the kind of darkness out of which anything a mind could conjure might spring; his fingers tightened around his heavy chrome torch which doubled as a club. On other trips he had used the top of a kerosene tin as a shield.

Nicholson switched his torch back on and the textured, earth-brown walls reappeared. The light he had inside the burrow was far easier to handle than the General Electric Watco spotlight that he used to move around the forest. It was a great clunker, with a globe as big as a saucer, connected by wires to a motorbike battery which was kept charged with the help of the school's handyman and cushioned inside an old army bag. It was one of Nicholson's most treasured possessions—a six-volt wet cell that had to be kept upright, which made it impossible to take down the wombat burrow. It had a purple bakelite handle like a gun handle—the whole package was a heavy load for a teenager running around the bush at night. On other occasions later in the year, in his quest to learn more about wombats, he would dig a hole into the side of the burrow into which he could stick his torch so he was able to work hands-free.

Wombats are the hobbits of the Australian bush, living underground and perceived as lazy and unadventurous. They are retiring solo folk, who give the impression of potential unfulfilled—neckless, stubborn, ferocious when cornered, intelligent, cute and mysterious. They don't, however, make burrows thinking of anyone else. Their tunnels are designed to fit their own bottoms snugly. It is part of a wombat's defence strategy that it can seal its home with an impenetrable posterior. Even so a wombat, unlike the teenage Nicholson, is able to execute a barrel roll with a twist that allows it to flip itself around a full 180 degrees. These creatures have the flexibility of a contortionist and are easily able to perform surprising acts of grace such as flicking their stumpy hind legs over their backs so they can scratch their ears. They are able to flatten themselves like dough under a rolling pin and slip through cracks less than ten centimetres high.

They can easily run 100 metres in under ten seconds. In fact they can maintain a speed of forty kilometres per hour for over 150 metres—only a handful of men on the planet are able to sustain thirty-six kilometres per hour for

100 metres. This speed is especially surprising given that scientists describe wombats as 'plantigrades'—animals that walk on the entire soles of their feet. Plantigrades, unlike many carnivores which run on the balls of their feet, are not programmed for racing. Wombats are also superb swimmers—I have seen them in Tasmania dog-paddling with their snouts barely visible above water.

Wombats are frighteningly efficient wrestlers, equipped with tough hides—a full one-centimetre-thick layer of skin—and a plate of bone, muscle and cartilage on their backs that enables them to squeeze under any intruder entering their tunnel and slam them against its roof. A predator prepared to take a bite out of a common wombat's backside would feel as though it had bitten the business end of a toilet brush. According to Barbara Triggs, one of Australia's leading experts on the animal, a wombat's fur at that point on its body is 200 microns in diameter, more like bristles—twice that of the coarsest human hair.

Wombat-like animals have lived in Australia for tens of millions of years: Tasmanian devils, Tasmanian tigers, marsupial lions, dingoes, foxes and almost certainly Aborigines have all been crushed to death in wombat burrows while searching for an easy feed. But these boltholes have saved lives too. On 26 October 1878, on Stringybark Creek, near the township of Mansfield, the trooper Thomas McIntyre fled from the

Kelly gang and hid in a wombat burrow and scribbled his account of the murders committed by the outlaws. As recently as 1997 a wombat burrow provided an escape from death for a Canberra woman who had fled naked from a pair of men who had raped her.

Wombats are one of the great survivors of the ravages that have been wrought on the Australian continent by climate change and humans. All animals and plants are divided into orders, families, genera and species. Wombats belong to the order Diprotodontia, marsupials that have two front incisors. The order includes kangaroos, possums and 'wombat-like creatures' such as koalas. The family that includes wombats is called the Vombatidae. In turn the Vombatidae is divided into two living genera—the bare-nosed or common wombats, and the hairy-nosed. Only one bare-nosed species exists today, although once there were several, and the scientific name of their genus is *Vombatus.* There are two hairy-nosed species— the northern and the southern—within the genus *Lasiorhinus.* Each species, however, is extremely different, and not just in respect to differences in habitat, burrows and food. The northern is the biggest of all, reaching weights of forty kilograms, the size of a small human teenager, and has a long snout compared to the southern's compacted muzzle. Hairy-nosed wombats have pointy ears while commons have dainty triangular ones. The southerns number a relatively comfortable 300,000, and there may be up to a million of the third species—the common wombat, though no-one knows for certain as commons have never been properly surveyed. The northerns, in contrast, are among the rarest animals in Australia and quite probably the rarest big mammal in the world. They are certainly the largest burrowing herbivores on the planet. The next biggest dirt-head vegetarians are the old-world porcupines, which come in at sixteen kilograms.

The plasma concentrations of thyroid hormones in wombats are the lowest recorded of any mammal, indicating a metabolism that is phenomenally efficient. Kangaroos are highly adapted low-intake feeders but still eat three times as much as southern hairy-nosed wombats. Wombat poo is the driest mammal poo on Earth because these animals are one of the most efficient consumers of water that mammal evolution has ever created. Even so a wombat can scull a drink with the best of them. Triggs has seen a wombat drink a litre of water, without pause, in just over three minutes. Once she observed another wombat sucking non-stop for eight minutes.

Wombats have also been popularised in the Australian consciousness as amiable duffers ever since Ruth Park wrote her enormously successful children's book *The Muddle-headed Wombat* in the mid-1950s. But the complexity of their brains means they are probably as intelligent as a carnivorous placental mammal and aspects of their senses are considered to be akin to those of primates. They are almost certainly the most intelligent of the world's marsupials.

At Timbertop, common wombats thrived everywhere except in the deepest and darkest of the fern gullies. The marsupials, Nicholson had already learned, loved burrowing into the banks of the creeks and rivers and into gullies and small hills. Even near the top of the mountain, 1200 metres above sea level, where only snow gums and heath grew, there were wombat colonies, contending for months each year with vast snow drifts.

Though it was close to freezing above ground, on this late April night in the tunnel the temperature was mild—Nicholson was to find that the subterranean temperature hardly changed, even when the forest at the burrow entrances was covered in snow. Flies hung on the wall of the tunnel, looking every bit like bats in a cave. During later expeditions he collected some of these hibernating insects in a tin and revived them in front of his friends back in his dormitory.

He could hear nothing apart from his own scrabblings, clangings and gruntings. Now he felt something hard and sharp dig painfully into his chest—it was a bone. He wiggled backwards until his hands were above the object and he grabbed it before dropping it into a tin held in front of him.

Wombats that die of natural causes invariably do so in their burrows and their skeletons are either buried by the next resident or pushed out during renovations. Dirt was sprinkling onto his back as if he was being seasoned for a roasting. In spite of the shower of sods he wriggled forward.

The tunnel opened up and after a couple of metres forked left and right. Nicholson turned right and after another two metres hit a second fork. He shone his torch to the right, dragging his body over an old nest of bracken. It was a dead end. The left fork curved around and he could see one tunnel too small to enter and, a little further along, a second nest. He backed up all the way to the first T-intersection and headed down the first left fork, which had a 90-degree bend in it. He found himself in the tightest bit of burrow he had yet encountered.

He could feel earth at the nape of his neck, and his shoulders had only a few centimetres clearance. More old bones dug into his chest as he scraped through. Down he went, over a number of dips and then, in an indentation in the wall of the burrow, he found a mummified carcass that looked fresh. In the cold, though, it didn't smell and Nicholson wondered at its age. He was now feeling chilled but unaware that he was so far underground that if he became stuck he would die there. No-one would ever find him.

Another four metres and the tunnel started to curve

around to the right. He began to feel and see dried fronds of bracken fern and strips of bark. There was still no noise. He turned the last corner awkwardly and there, less than a metre in front of him, was a wombat lying in its nest. It was laid out on its stomach, legs sprawled behind it. The chamber where it lay was the size of a small couch and the first airy space Nicholson had seen that night. He felt a rush of fear and exhilaration. His hand tightened on his torch and both he and the wombat exchanged a stare of shock. Never before, in recorded history, had a wombat and a human had such an encounter.

Nicholson waited to see its reaction. It looked at him as if to say 'what the hell are you?' and made a strange grunt that Nicholson instinctively imitated. The noise seemed to calm the animal. Somehow that look of confusion on its face reassured Nicholson he wasn't going to be attacked after all. After a while it got on with its business of scratching, digging and stretching as if the nervous boy was accepted. Nicholson, curled in a foetal position, kept on repeating his imitative grunt until it was time to back out and head for home. He swore to himself, though, that he would be back.

Outside the air was cold on his sweat and an autumn breeze was ruffling the silhouetted trees. Nicholson felt euphoric; it was as if the forest was opening up before him and the wilderness was his.

Chapter 2

SECRET LIVES

The burrow is a personal home containing usually one, but sometimes two, adult wombats at one time...I have never seen wombats actually mating. The breeding season extends from about the end of March until June. The mother wombat usually has only one young, or very rarely two.

PETER NICHOLSON

All of Geelong Grammar's fifteen-year-olds are sent to Timbertop for a year in the bush before returning to the main campus to complete their final two years of schooling. Nicholson hailed from Canberra and to get to Timbertop had travelled on various trains and buses. Like all the other students, he arrived with a suitcase filled with walking boots, old clothes, tent, sleeping-bag and a backpack. Nicholson's backpack was a Yukon, with two timber rails on either side, a couple of hooks and a bit of canvas lashed between. In his bag he also had traps that his Dad had given him, and within his first few days had started catching marsupial mice.

There were 135 boys at the school—about twelve students to each of the huts (modelled on old workmen's buildings and called units). The beds were all side by side and windows opened out to the forest. There was no heating other than the boiler and a big open fire in a communal room that doubled as a study. If the boiler went out the boys went cold and so did the water. Eating took place in a big dining hall and virtually the whole place was run by the students, who were responsible for a huge number of chores, which were supervised by the masters.

The boy in the next bed, Jim Palmer, didn't stir when Nicholson returned from wombatting. A few days later, however, Nicholson was called up and made to stand outside the office of the housemaster, Hugh Montgomery.

Montgomery's nickname was Basher and he was famous for the way he meted out justice. Being called up to his office was enough to make boys tremble. Montgomery had a huge responsibility on his shoulders. On the first day of the 1960 academic year at Timbertop one of the students disappeared under the milk-coloured waters of the school dam. His body was not found until late that night and, although the coroner cleared the staff of any negligence, Montgomery, according to those who knew him, bore that scar until his death. Some weeks after this tragedy he summoned Nicholson into his office.

'Rules,' Montgomery said slowly and deliberately to the boy, stretching the word like a rubber band, 'are made for the majority. Don't lead anyone astray who doesn't know what they are doing.' It was a cryptic warning that Nicholson interpreted as a possible green light for his wanderings. Montgomery was cutting Nicholson some rope.

Timbertop had been open for only seven years when Nicholson arrived. Five years after he left, it reached the peak of its fame when a young Prince Charles spent most of 1966 there. There were no telephones for boys to contact their parents—independence, hard work and a love of the bush were the values to be instilled into the boys. The only remedy for homesickness was that each week, on a Sunday evening, every student had to write a letter to his parents and hand it in to the masters. In none of these did Nicholson mention that he had begun to venture deep inside the network of tunnels that make up a wombat burrow.

Nicholson had first become interested in wombats after seeing the creatures in the hills behind his home in Canberra. His father was Dr Alexander John Nicholson—chief of the CSIRO's Division of Entomology through World War II and into the 1960s. Dr Nicholson moved in the small, elite intellectual circles of Canberra in the postwar years. Peter grew up in an environment where some of Australia's most distinguished scientists, politicians and artists would drop in without warning to spend an afternoon or evening with his parents. Australia's most famous physicist, Sir Mark Oliphant, was a close friend of his father. One evening Oliphant, who as a senior member of the Manhattan Project played a key role in the development of the nuclear bomb, showed the Nicholson family a 'newfangled' device he had brought back from the United States. It was called a blender and Oliphant planned to make an eggflip—only he forgot to put the top on it and sprayed the concoction all over the ceiling.

On another evening Antarctic explorer Sir Douglas Mawson came to the Nicholson home for dinner. Peter was about five years old and was told to listen and not be heard. All the men were standing around the fireplace yarning and drinking whisky while the boy looked on from behind the couch.

A. J. Nicholson was a quiet Englishman, who graduated

in zoology after World War I had started and was sent to the front at Ypres in Belgium as an officer in the Royal Artillery. In 1924 he came out to Australia and took a job at the University of Sydney. He spent his weekends at places such as Palm Beach, collecting butterflies and beetles. There was always a little specimen bottle in his pocket; a butterfly net and magnifying glass would be close at hand. On holidays he even set up devices so he could photograph insects with a remote control while he read whodunits (which he loved).

Nicholson's mother, Phyllis Jarret, was a multidisciplinary scientist and teacher. At the University of Melbourne she wrote her masters thesis on the Aboriginal use of fire and later worked with Professor John Mulvaney—Australia's most eminent prehistorian. Together with Mulvaney she assisted with the early work at Lake Mungo, today a world-heritage location that boasts some of the oldest modern human remains on the planet. Apart from being a gifted scientist she was an adventurer and thrill-seeker. She was a glider pilot in England and Germany and had travelled to the Kerguelen Islands in the sub-Antarctic. She met Peter's father when she was working at the CSIRO. A friend of Nicholson's initiated an open challenge to find the woman who could seduce the insect-obsessed scientist. The pair fell in love and she collected her prize, a whisky decanter, at the wedding.

There were many nights and days when Peter Nicholson went back to the burrow where he had found his friendly wombat. He soon discovered an area down another, more capacious hole which was easily excavated and enlarged. One cavern was so big that a group of boys once clambered down and hid inside it.

Peter began to make copious notes about the wombats and their secret lives. For the remainder of 1960 he continued tunnelling and excavating, measuring and recording all that he found. More than four decades later wombat scientists throughout Australia look back in awe at his achievements. By sitting for hours silently watching them, he learned how wombats dug their burrows. He enjoyed observing the social interaction between these animals that most researchers assumed were loners. He refined the etiquette required to journey down a tunnel without causing offence to its owner—a constant stream of friendly grunts 'hhhmmmpph, hhhhmmmmppph' and a slow, respectful approach. He discovered that, rather than always sleeping inside their burrows, wombats were extraordinarily active, scratching and building nests. He recorded what they ate—roots, fungi and grasses. He even collected the ticks that feasted on the creatures, jotting that wombats 'are the host of a large blood sucking tick, many of which I collected by finding replete ones which had fallen off in the burrow'. His Dad would have been pleased.

He even befriended an albino wombat, and observed how this sun-shy creature coped with its genetic disorder. It was the only wombat he observed closely that came out *only* at night. In the middle of winter he experimented with how much snow a wombat could dig through to reach the outside world, discovering that a two-metre drift posed no challenge whatsoever. Even through the roughest ground a wombat can excavate at least a metre of burrow in just a few hours, using its blade-like teeth, massive flat skull, short strong legs and stubborn nature.

In the coldest months of the year, while the rest of the boys huddled around the fire in their dorm, Peter monitored feeding patterns and learnt that in winter wombats emerge every two to three days but otherwise stay in the deepest part of their tunnels. Becoming more and more confident as each week passed he even felt safe enough to escape one evening after lights out and make the thirty-kilometre round trip to the Mount Buller ski resort. His plan was to say hello to the sister of one of his friends who was working there. He saw the girl, made his greetings, then arrived back at Timbertop just as the sky was turning grey and his rollcall was under way.

The real adventure, however, was not girls: it was tracking wombats as they barrelled across the snow plains. He was able to recognise their signs the way other boys spotted coins dropped on the ground. One of the clearest giveaways of a resident wombat was a sapling coated in dry mud—wombats have a great love of scratching their gloriously luxuriant behinds against a tree. One morning he saw a wombat do this for twenty minutes without a rest.

His work resulted in the first ever measurements of wombat burrows. He would drive a peg into the floor of a tunnel and stretch string between the markers. The cord was then measured and angles determined with the help of a protractor. Slopes were judged on a qualitative basis only—by

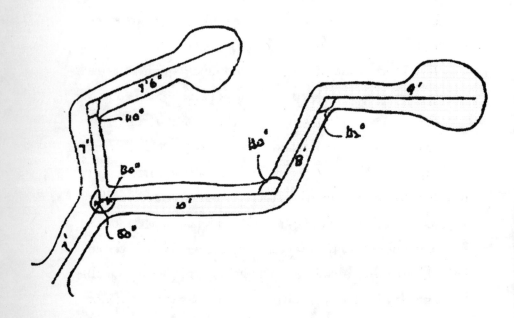

Peter Nicholson mapped his burrows by pegging out rope and measuring the angles. He was the first person to do so.

how hard it was to crawl up or down them. All of his wombat maps were then sketched out in notebooks. When biologists with framed doctorates on their office walls followed up Nicholson's work, using bulldozers to take the lid off the wombat world, they merely confirmed that the schoolboy's findings were remarkably accurate.

Wombatting, Nicholson had discovered, was something that gave him precious time on his own. The middle of the night and weekends were about the only times he had free— during the week there were cross-country runs, classes and jobs such as wood-chopping, collecting kindling, cleaning boilers, and the dreaded task of tending the school's fly traps. Occasionally a friend accompanied him but more often than not he headed off into the forest alone.

It was on the far side of Mount Timbertop, down on the Howqua River, that Nicholson had his two most dangerous wombat encounters. It was now spring and he had been at the school for about six months. On the Howqua the soils were sandy and unstable, which made Peter extremely nervous, but it didn't stop him from carefully exploring underground. He was now confident of his bush skills and knew which burrows he could enter relatively safely. During the winter he had seen several burrows that had experienced huge cave-ins and in all but one of these it appeared that the wombats had not escaped.

The Howqua was so close he could hardly hear himself think over the roar of its rapids. He found a new burrow, dropped onto his knees and commando-crawled inside its entrance. With a few deft wriggles his feet disappeared into the darkness; he might as well have vanished from the forest. He negotiated a rollercoaster-like hump inside the entrance and then continued down, down, through a puddle in a dip before he chose a left fork.

It was then he heard a sound he had not encountered before. At first he thought it was an echo of the river. It got louder. Out of the darkness, still far away, came a scrabbling noise—like a cockroach scuttling on paper. It grew more and more ominous until Nicholson's entire field of vision was suddenly filled with saliva and fangs. His ears hurt from the growling, and without giving his body any instructions he was caterpillaring backwards at full wriggle, shield up, just holding back the startled, enraged wild dog. Soon he was back above ground and away from the wild creature.

A few weekends later, Nicholson and some friends were back on the Howqua. They were fishing close to the shack of an old prospector named Fred Fry, who was renowned for being able to pull a trout out of the river with a grasshopper on a bent nail. He was always willing to give an ear to the boys passing through on their hikes and would often invite them in. 'Do you feel like a fish?' he would say before going down to the river and pulling one out as if it were already hanging on the line.

There was a big burrow on the riverbank near Fry's hut, in which Nicholson had disturbed, on a previous trip, a red-bellied black snake. It was always cool down a burrow and fortunately cold snakes are not very active. It wasn't completely coiled up—and would have been more worried about the boy than he was about it. On another day while visiting Fry he stepped over a log and his foot landed on a black snake, a genuinely gross, rubbery feeling that Nicholson has never forgotten.

Leaving his friends fishing, Nicholson went into the new burrow making his wombat noises. Once inside he eyeballed a big angry female and immediately knew he wasn't welcome, no matter how well he spoke wombat. She charged at him ferociously, hissing and grunting, as though she was prepared to bulldoze him straight out of her hole. Once again Nicholson found himself beating an awkward retreat, one hand holding his torch and the other ready to defend himself.

As he arrived back home that night, his hair matted with dirt, Nicholson had no inkling of the research benefits of his crazy adventures. He went on exploring and in time his understanding of the behaviour of wombats became so great that he was familiar with the comings and goings at a dozen burrows and knew the residents' behaviour at at least two of these tunnels.

Whenever he went past one of his burrows, or when he found a new entrance, he would flatten the dirt across the front with his hand so when he came back he could see how many times the inhabitants had been in and out, or whether there was a dog in the burrow.

As the end of 1960 approached, Nicholson was still under the impression that, with the exception of a few close friends, no-one knew about his wombatting. That was before Montgomery summoned him again. The boy feared the worst. His anxiety deepened when he was shown into the house-master's office and the Geelong Grammar senior science master, Ken Mappin, was there.

'Show Mr Mappin your wombatting work, Nicholson,' Montgomery said lightly.

'Sir?' Nicholson replied, acting dumb.

'Just show him, Nicholson.'

The pair of them headed off together, across the creek and through the scrub to the burrow that was home to the friendly wombat. He left Mappin downwind of the burrow, about twenty metres from the entrance. The boy broke out into a 'hhhmmpphh, hhhmmmpphh, hhhhmmpphh'. The master, sitting under a tree, was bemused at these strange antics. After several minutes a shadow appeared down the tunnel and a wombat popped out, clearly recognising Nicholson. Mappin was stunned and remained silent as Nicholson reeled off fact after fact about the furry boulder of an animal plodding around his legs. Nicholson recounted the story of how he had obtained several skeletons' worth of bones and filled notepads with behavioural data. He even revealed that he had maps of the burrows.

The following year when Nicholson was back at Geelong he was approached by the science master. 'Nicholson,' Mappin said, 'we need something entered in the Victorian science talent quest.'

Early drafts of a paper were pulled together, then, at home in Canberra just before Christmas 1961, Nicholson began to write his story in full. He knew he had done something that had set him apart from all other boys his age. His exploits were now legendary at the school and, through his parents, his odd achievements were even being talked about by scientists at some of the most prestigious academic establishments in the nation. Skeletal material he had collected had been sent to the CSIRO's Division of Wildlife and Ecology. After a few introductory scribbles, Nicholson cut to the chase. 'During 1960, while I was at Timbertop, I had a wonderful opportunity to do what I had always wanted to do—to study wombats in their natural surroundings, and to explore their underground burrows.'

He did not know its significance but he had begun writing a scientific paper, detailing for the first time the secret life of wombats. His mother helped him proofread it but to her credit allowed the boy his voice.

I first came across the Nicholson story myself in 1995 when I was in south-western New South Wales at a town called Wentworth to investigate the discovery of a population of southern hairy-nosed wombats. It had been a frustrating day—wombats are notoriously elusive and the species we were looking for was also very rare in that area, with perhaps only a few individuals in the entire state. We were in a wheat field at dusk and it was as if the native inhabitants of this environment had silently vanished. We could see their burrows, their poo and their footprints, but no wombats.

The scientists accompanying us—one was Dr Linda Gibson, a mammalogist from the Australian Museum—were almost certain that the animals were hiding underground, probably because we were there. I remember looking down a burrow. Within a metre or two its branching tunnels disappeared into sudden darkness. The dimness spooked me because once while diving I had thought a friend had drowned as he attempted to snorkel through an underwater tunnel. When I began thinking he was stuck I had the sickening feeling of realising that I may not have the courage to go down and pull him out. I had nightmares about the incident for months.

Like most people, I won't put my body into any dark, unknown place that could harbour something with teeth, fangs or poisonous spines. I once joined some New South Wales cavers, hundreds of metres along a cavern, to write a piece about the bizarre discovery of a Brett Whiteley signature in a deep prohibited part of the Jenolan cave system. Whiteley, one of the country's finest artists, had left the signature as a ten-year-old while on a trip with his mother. I knew when I saw his name that I would never be brave enough to come down to such a place on my own.

As we walked back to our cars from the wheat field in Wentworth, having given up looking for wombats, the image of the burrow entrance played on my mind. 'Does anyone know what is down wombat burrows?' I asked Linda. 'Has anyone researched them?'

Her answer shocked me. 'The best study ever done on wombat burrows was by a schoolboy from Timbertop,' she said.

As soon as I was back in Sydney I decided to track down the paper. A few calls later I was talking to Michael Collins Persse, a remarkable educator who has worked at Geelong Grammar since 1955. He told me all about Peter Nicholson. Collins Persse also taught Prince Charles while he was at the school and maintains a friendship with its most famous student more than three decades later. Collins Persse had taught Nicholson English, history and geography, and had acted as his godfather at the school. His memories of the boy he called Peter John were so clear it was as if he had been waiting for my call. Nicholson, Collins Persse told me, had been an amazingly gifted young man with a very special personality and a love of wildlife. He promised to dig the scientific paper out of the school archives and send me a copy. Within an hour a fax had arrived and I found myself all agog by its contents.

Nearly every book on marsupials that deals with wombats cites the Nicholson paper. In 1988 Barbara Triggs wrote in her book *The Wombat* that Nicholson's work remains still 'one of the most useful "in depth" studies of wombats that has been published'.

As the years have passed the boy's exploits have become legendary. The paper won Nicholson cult status among wombat scientists and marsupial experts alike—generations of first-year biology students at the University of New South Wales have been taught about the wombat boy by awestruck professors.

Peter Nicholson's paper is a beautiful piece of writing— an inspired mixture of keen observation and good biological science. 'The wombat has powerful long claws and the front paws are hollowed out rather like a hand. With these it digs deep burrows into the hillside or on flat country. The longest burrow I ever explored was about sixty feet, not counting the network of tunnels. A plan of an actual burrow is shown in the sketch.'

A reader today can still understand what a great adventure this must have been for a secondary-school student: 'I have followed or tracked wombats up and down slopes for more than two miles. When a wombat is travelling with a purpose it is very hard to keep up with him and remain unseen. I used a small yukon pack toboggan and only then could I keep up with the wombat. If you chase a wombat it is impossible to catch it as it moves up or down a slope with equal ease and will disappear down any burrow.'

And there are thrilling moments when Nicholson gets very close to these wild creatures: 'Soon I learned that they were usually friendly and very inquisitive but not until second term did I start in earnest to try to make friends with one. I picked a fairly young wombat and spent an hour each day with it. This time was never wasted as he usually gave me some demonstration of digging or burrow life. I always had a torch with me but never pointed it directly at him, and it always contained, on these occasions, dull batteries. For quite long periods the torch was off so that he could examine me. Occasionally he would come up to me and sniff my arms and examine my face and hair inquisitively while I imitated his friendly grunt.'

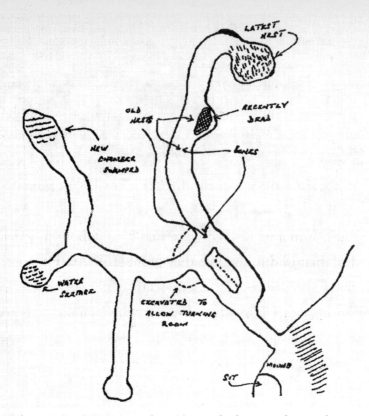

LATEST
NEST

OLD
NESTS

RECENTLY
DEAD

NEW
CHAMBER
SHELVED

LANES

WATER
SEEPAGE

EXCAVATED TO
ALLOW TURNING
ROOM

MOUND

SIT

Nicholson spent much of 1960 exploring this complex burrow and once took a group of friends down into its labyrinthine network.

Nicholson's research was to give him a wisdom beyond his years: 'My study, conducted over a period of a year, was incomplete, but it did supply me with most of the information which I had set out to find out. It also taught me that you cannot say positively what such an intelligent animal will do. He will have certain habits but, as he is at least as intelligent as a dog, he is unpredictable.'

It was his account of being chased out of the burrow that most captured my imagination. 'Some communities of wombats were less friendly than others and these near a camp where there were dogs were definitely hostile,' he wrote. 'One female wombat living on the Howqua River bank, possibly with young, chased me out of the burrow by grunting and advancing at me. This is the only time I have been chased out by a wombat.'

At that moment I resolved to find P. J. Nicholson—what kind of man did a boy like that grow into? After a search through the phone book, and a few baffled answers from other P. Nicholsons, I located him. After many phone calls we arranged to meet at his Sydney home. I was surprised at how young he looked—he has no grey hair and appears fit and youthful. He laughs often and loudly and I liked him immediately. His wombat research was something that had begun and ended while he was at Timbertop. Never again after 1960 did he go down a burrow. I asked him why he didn't continue to study the animal. 'Why would I?' he replied. 'I had found out everything I wanted to know about them.'

Nicholson read economics after leaving school and became a successful businessman. His home is on the harbour, with its own little private beach and a 100-metre escalator that transports visitors from the road, down an escarpment, to his verandah. He remains a passionate observer of all forms of life in the natural world. He still carries a magnifying glass and his family tease him about his strange ability to make all kinds of animals relax in his presence simply by imitating them. One of his favourite tricks is to mimic the strange head-flicking movement of the eastern water dragons that live around his home. Over the years all kinds of people have sought out Nicholson, including scientists from overseas who have heard of his exploits. Every year at least one person contacts him about his research. In the 1960s the Australian artist Clifton Pugh helped launch a resurgence in wombat popularity and read the teenager's scientific paper. Pugh and his family raised around a dozen orphaned wombats in outer Melbourne.

'Whatever I did I always thought that it had been done before,' Nicholson said. 'It's a tragedy that it hadn't and that I am still considered an expert on wombats. The burrows were there and I just went further and further.'

When the masters at Geelong Grammar saw the paper Nicholson had written during his holidays they agreed that it would be sent to the 1962 statewide Science Talent Quest, which would be judged in Wilson Hall at the University of Melbourne. Over 150 projects were entered, representing in excess of 300 students, including six from Geelong Grammar. On Friday 22 June and again the next morning students filled the building, carting in their massive contraptions: hovercrafts, chemistry experiments and every kind of whistling, boiling, bubbling machine imaginable. Nicholson arrived with a manila folder and his wombat skull. He was stunned to discover when he arrived that the precis for his entry was pinned to the door of the hall and that he was a winner.

His precis read: 'Little is known about Australia's burrowing marsupial the wombat, other than what has been studied of it in captivity or by open-cutting the burrows. My study of it has been made in its natural surroundings by crawling down burrows and making friends with the inhabitants.'

What Nicholson didn't know as he left Timbertop after his year of wombat research, was that he himself had answered a question posed at the end of the eighteenth century by another curious young man—the explorer George Bass.

Chapter 3

THE WOMBACH

After about three months of knowing me he followed me out of the burrow as I was leaving it. I sat down near his sit and he in it. The day was overcast and very dull. He then came up to me and examined me very closely, putting his forepaws on my legs and sniffing up and down my legs. After this he would usually follow me out on a dull day. I never attempted to feed him and it seemed he was only inquisitive. He gave the impression of being an intelligent, one-track-mind person. He used to love to be scratched.

PETER NICHOLSON

Bass Strait is a museum of climate change, a place where both land and life have been cast away from the rest of the world. Over 120 pieces of continental Australia, ranging in size from battered rocks poking just above the surf to the 200,000-hectare Flinders Island, were surrounded by ocean when the sea level rose at the end of the last ice age, around 10,000 years ago. It is a beautiful part of the world that can turn treacherous when a storm slams into its shallow seas.

On maps, Wilsons Promontory in southern Victoria looks like a witch's finger beckoning to the stepping-stone trail of islands that stretch across Bass Strait. Until 10,000 years ago animals and people crossed this land bridge between Tasmania and the mainland. But slowly and inexorably over several thousand years, as the planet warmed, this land became marsh, marsh became lakes, and lakes became sea.

Entire ecosystems, which included people and wombats, were left stuck. The people succumbed to isolation, disease and the genetic consequences of a small population soon after the land bridge was destroyed but many strange animals survived. Yet eighteenth-century explorers, seeking shortcuts between Great Britain and the new colony in Port Jackson, made life for these creatures increasingly difficult. The First Fleet rounded the southern extreme of Van Diemen's Land before sailing up the east coast of Australia. In the first ten years of settlement, the seaway south of Tasmania was the

route of choice for visitors to the new colony. The only alter-
native was to traverse the tropical seas to the north of the
continent, considered even more hazardous.

I have flown low over the whitecaps, just above the
albatrosses, across these islands, breathing a sigh of relief every
time a lump of land appeared below the wings of the Cessna.
To see the island groups of Bass Strait from the air, first the
Kent Group and then the Furneaux Group, is to appreciate
what greenhouse-induced loneliness must really feel like. It
also conveys a sense of how dramatic the reappearance of
humans must have been for animals such as the wombat.

Even a decade after the arrival of Europeans in Sydney,
not one soul from the northern hemisphere had recorded the
presence of a wombat. This is not as surprising as it sounds.
Coastal Sydney probably never had many wombats. And few
people ventured into the forest at night, when these creatures
are most active. Unlike kangaroos, wombats are not found in
great bounding mobs. But in February 1797 the *Sydney Cove*
was caught in an easterly gale off the north-east tip of
Tasmania and the ship was run ashore by her eighty-year-old
captain. The *Sydney Cove* had hit what the fifty-five crew would
name Preservation Island. Luckily for the survivors, a large, fat
mammal thrived on the 200-hectare outcrop in huge
numbers. Unused to people, they could be clubbed on the
head with ease, providing a ready source of meat. It was the

first time Europeans encountered wombats. Millennia had passed on these islands since the ancestors of these wombats were hunted by ancient Aborigines.

A longboat was prepared and eighteen of the *Sydney Cove's* crew were sent on a hellish journey to civilisation. Only three men were alive by the time they were rescued near Coalcliff, south of Sydney. The *Francis* was dispatched immediately to rescue those waiting on Preservation Island. On 16 February 1798 the *Francis*, with Matthew Flinders aboard, returned to the strait, this time to salvage the cargo—7000 gallons of rum. While this job was being done Flinders visited the nearby Cape Barren Island. The sailors with him killed a number of wombats and also captured a living specimen, a female. On its voyage from the Furneaux islands it ate nothing except rice forced down its throat. On 9 March when the *Francis* docked back in Sydney, this starving creature was presented to Governor Hunter.

While these maritime dramas were under way the first European reference to a 'whom-batt' was made in a diary entry. It was 26 January 1798, exactly ten years since Phillip hoisted the Union Jack. The entry was written by John Price, a servant of Governor John Hunter, who had travelled to the Blue Mountains with a former convict, John Wilson. Wilson's life is testimony to how quickly a place can absorb and recreate a human being. He was transported as a convict with the First Fleet, for the theft of nine yards of cotton cloth, but four years after arriving in Sydney he was freed. He fled the confines of the fledgling city by the harbour and took up with the Aborigines, surviving on the periphery of the colony. Australia has a long tradition of eccentric bushmen and Wilson was among the first. He was also one of the most radical. Named Bun-bo-e by Aborigines, he was heavily scarred with tribal markings and at times wore nothing but kangaroo skins. He explored a large slab of the territory within 150 kilometres of Sydney and was one of the few Europeans who felt at home in this new world of strange animals, bushfires and fiercely rugged bush.

On 24 January, Wilson, Price and their party left Mount Hunter and followed the Nepean River. The expedition had a bizarre purpose. Hunter sent them out to end rumours that a colony of free white people was living a life of ease and luxury 300 kilometres north of Sydney. By the end of 26 January the explorers had travelled, by their own count, thirty-four miles and Price had guaranteed himself a spot in Australian history by recording for the first time the existence of three iconic Australian animals: the wombat, the koala and the lyrebird.

'We saw several sorts of dung of different animals,' Price wrote, 'one of which Wilson called a Whom-batt, which is an animal about 20 inches high, with short legs and a thick body with a large head, round ears, and very small eyes, is very fat and has much the appearance of a badger. There is another animal which the natives call a cullawine, which much resembles the sloths in America. Here I shot a bird about the size of a pheasant, but the tail of it very much resembles a peacock, with two large, long feathers, which are white, orange and lead colour, and black at the ends; its body betwixt a brown and green; brown under its neck and black upon his head; black legs and very long claws.'

Six months later, on 5 August 1798, John Hunter sat down at his desk in Sydney and wrote a letter to the great botanist Sir Joseph Banks, informing him that an 'unknown creature' had been discovered. He was fascinated by the mammal Flinders had brought back to Sydney, even though it died of starvation after refusing to eat for more than six weeks. He knew that Banks' interest in the strange animals of New Holland had remained undiminished in spite of the fact that nearly three decades had passed since his great voyages of discovery with Captain James Cook. A proud but zoologically confused governor declared himself unequal to the task of a correct description of the 'Uncommon Animal'. Preserved in spirits, minus its brain and intestines, it was dispatched from the colony to England for the 'inspection of the learned members of the Literary and Philosophical Society of Newcastle upon Tyne'. Unaware of its need to burrow and its preference for darkness, Hunter recorded that in its pitiful life in captivity it fled underneath shrubs whenever it was taken out of its box. '[It] was exposed in a small place enclosed,' he wrote, 'where it received in the day time, the benefit of the warmth of the sun, which however it did not seem to enjoy.'

He observed that its size was nearly that of a badger, 'a species of which we supposed it to be by the dexterity with which it would bury itself in the Earth by means of its fore paws.' Today, in parts of Tasmania and in the forests north of Sydney, wombats are still known as badgers. The governor also noted its similarity to bears, that it was not carnivorous and that its dentition was strikingly like that of the kangaroo. 'This animal has lately been discovered to be an inhabitant of the interior of this country also.' Hunter told Banks, 'its flesh is delicate meat—the Mountain Natives call it Wombach this one is a female and has the false belly for the security of the young'. But the shape of the creature stretched the administrator's imagination. 'There is something uncommon in the make of its hind parts, from the hip joint the posteriors do not sound off like most other animals, but fall suddenly down quite flat in a sloping direction.'

On 13 September 1798 Banks noted his receipt of Hunter's letter: 'A large animal between a bear and a badger has been discovered in large numbers.' It must have been an astonishing letter for Banks to read in London. Hunter followed his account of the Wombach with a description of another baffling animal from New South Wales. 'An amphibious animal of the mole kind—found in the fresh-water lakes, its size is about that of a small cat, or longer very considerably than the Sand Mole; it inhabits the banks of these lakes, it has exactly the bill of a Duck, probably feeds in muddy places in the same way.'

To read such words dramatically highlights how the world has grown smaller. It also demonstrates what an open book the planet was for European explorers. The closest we can get to such eighteenth-century wonder is our amazement at mobile phones with built-in GPS systems or colour tele-visions that fit into the palm of a hand. And Hunter's letter might have been more shocking: he did not know that the platypus lays eggs. Maybe, though, Banks understood that the continent he had discovered with Cook would yield such biological wonders as it was explored—after all he was on board the *Endeavour* when the first sighting of a kangaroo was recorded by a European on 22 June 1770. Three days later Banks saw the confounding creature and wrote: 'In gathering plants today I myself had the good fortune to see the beast so much talked of, tho but imperfectly; he was not only like a greyhound in size and running but had a long tail, as long as any greyhounds; what to liken him to I could not tell, nothing certainly that I have seen at all resembles him.'

Governor Hunter's wombat drawing of 1798, the first of its kind, was the basis for this engraving, reproduced in David Collins' An account of the English Colony in New South Wales in 1802.

By the time Cook's voyage to New Holland was over at least 616 new animal species had been discovered, including twenty-two mammals, ninety-three birds, fourteen reptiles, sixty-five fishes, 244 insects and a sponge. An analysis of the discoveries of Cook's voyage, prepared by the Royal Zoological Society of New South Wales, puts the extent of the scientific discoveries made by Cook and Banks into perspective. As late as 1758 in the tenth edition of Linnaeus's *Systema Naturae* there were, in the entire known planet, only 184 mammal species,

554 birds, 218 amphibia, 378 fishes, 2110 insects and 936 worms—a grand total of 4380 animal species.

And yet, in spite of the perception that it was Cook who opened Australia up to Europeans, by the time he arrived nearly a hundred animal species were already known from earlier explorations. Europeans had been struggling for more than 160 years, since the first Dutch sailor made it ashore, to come to terms with the wildlife oddities that 40 million years of geographic isolation had presented. Almost everything the early explorers saw that was endemic to Australia was almost too strange, and could only be made sense of in terms of some existing animal grouping from elsewhere in the world. In 1699 when William Dampier made his second voyage to Australia, he mistook the wallabies he saw for raccoons and confused a dugong carcass with a hippopotamus.

'Of the sharks we caught a great many, which our Men ate very savourily,' Dampier wrote of his journey to the Western Australian coast. 'Among them we caught one which was 11 Foot long. The space between its Eyes was 20 inches, and 18 Inches from one Corner of its Mouth to the other. Its Maw was like a Leather Sack, very thick and so tough that a sharp Knife could scarce cut it: In which we found the Head and Boans of a Hippopotamus; the hairy lips of which were still sound and not putrified, and the Jaw was also firm, out of which we pluckt a great many teeth.'

Dampier's description of a shingleback lizard also provides a stunning glimpse into how confusing Australian animals were to northern hemisphere eyes: 'At the rump, instead of the Tail there, they had a stump of a Tail, which appeared like another Head; but not really such, being without Mouth or Eyes: yet this Creature seem'd by this means to have a Head at each end…the legs also seem'd, all 4 of them, to be Fore-legs, being all alike in Shape and Length, and seeming by the Joints and Bending to be made as if they were to go indifferently either Head or Tail foremost.'

By the time of Dampier's voyage Europeans had known about marsupials for two centuries, since Vincente Pinzón found an opossum with pouch young in the land now known as Brazil. On returning to Spain in the early 1500s he 'presented the incredible mother' at the court of Ferdinand and Isabella, who put their hands into the pouch and marvelled at 'so strange a contrivance of nature'.

Even to an Australian like myself, who has spent his entire life around marsupials, the first close look at a pouch is a baffling experience. In February 2001, I was at Taronga Zoo in Sydney and was given the opportunity to touch the pouch of Walcha, a female wombat which had been anaesthetised so that her fertility could be assessed. Wombats are classified by zoo staff as 'hazardous'—a formal label only one step below the 'dangerous' tag applied to lions, tigers and bears.

'Dangerous' means an animal is capable of killing a person, 'hazardous' that serious injury is possible. One of the zoo's wombats, a ferocious male called Wallace, can jump nearly a metre into the air and has razor-sharp grazing teeth.

Walcha had to be tackled from behind and held around her shoulders in order to keep her still for a gas mask to be fitted over her muzzle. She attacked the mask, striking the plastic with viper-like blows of her jaw. As the gas started to take effect her writhing slowed until she resembled a huge flat

Taronga zookeeper Terry Boylan gives Walcha a bear hug in preparation for her pouch examination.

rug. Once she was unconscious the vets began swabbing, measuring her pouch, removing blood and examining her vagina, including her clitoris. After the check-up was complete and before she was taken off the gas I was able to feel inside Walcha's pouch. It was furry, slimy and warm and went deeper than my few fingers felt brave enough to explore. A wombat's pouch opens about ten centimetres from its birth canal. The opening was about the size of a 20-cent piece and her nipples were just inside. I couldn't help but wonder at how my branch of the mammal tree had diverged from that of the wombat's. No wonder Ferdinand and Isabella were so shocked by the 'incredible mother'—five centuries later I walked away from Walcha beguiled by what I had seen.

At the end of October 1798, two months after Hunter wrote to Banks, the naturalist George Bass was landed in the Furneaux Group while Matthew Flinders in the *Norfolk* sounded the depths of channels between the islands. Their mission was to determine whether Tasmania—or as it was then known, Van Diemen's Land—was indeed an island. Some time between 20 October 1798 and 31 October Bass, probably on Cape Barren Island, made the first detailed anatomical description of the wombat.

At twenty-five-odd tonnes the *Norfolk* was a relatively

small ship that leaked extensively on her maiden voyage, but for Bass she must have seemed like a luxury liner. Less than a year earlier, at twenty-seven years of age, he had explored this region in *Tom Thumb*, a six-oared whaleboat only five metres long. For that era he was a big man—180 centimetres tall—and he and Flinders were firm friends. 'Together,' writes Tim Flannery, editor of Matthew Flinders' *Terra Australis*, 'these young men would carry out some of the most audacious voyages ever attempted in the history of Australian exploration.'

The days that Bass shared with Flinders in the Furneaux Group must have been truly amazing. Imagine what it would have been like for Bass to see the following sight as recorded by his colleague, Flinders: 'A large flock of gannets was observed at daylight, to issue out of the great bight to the southward; and they were followed by such a number of sooty petrels as we had never seen equalled. There was a stream from fifty to eighty yards in depth, and of three hundred yards, or more, in breadth; the birds were not scattered, but flying as compactly as a free movement of their wings seemed to allow; and during a full hour and a half, this stream of petrels continued to pass without interruption, at a rate little inferior to the swiftness of the pidgeon. On the lowest computation, I think the number could not have been less than a hundred millions.'

As the *Sydney Cove* survivors had found before Bass, wombats lived on these islands in enormous numbers and, because they were inexperienced in the ways of people, the marsupials were incredibly tame. The explorers were visiting a biological paradise where animals knew no fear because millennia without humans had erased any memory of their predatoriness.

Bass' account of his encounters with wombats is still held with Sir Joseph Banks' papers but is not dated or signed so we have no precise idea when it was written. Experts, however, have studied the handwriting and are almost certain that the correspondence was penned by Bass. It is in this account that we first see the new animal given its modern pronunciation: 'When the first that was brought to Port Jackson, was shown to the natives all of them were ignorant of it but a mountain native. He declared it to be an inhabitant of the blue mountains or that range of mountains which be immediately at the back of the settlement; and that there its name was Wom-bat.'

Other Aboriginal names used for the new creature that crop up in correspondence and diaries of the time include 'womat' and 'womback'. The fact is, though, that Australia was home to hundreds of distinct languages at the time of occupation by Europeans. The only reason we are left with the name 'wombat' is because the Aboriginal man, who happened to be in Sydney the day that the first Tasmanian specimen arrived, called it that. Aborigines throughout the continent had an immense variety of names for wombats. Countless stories were also told around Australia, before Europeans arrived, about how the wombat ended up being the kind of animal he is.

In Tasmania one name for the wombat is 'Publedina'. According to a story recorded in 1830 by the Cottons, a settler family, the Publedina was originally called the Drogerdy. In 1979 Jackson Cotton published a series of stories about animals that his ancestors had recorded. In 1997 these stories were again printed in a beautiful book called *Taraba*, which offers a very rare glimpse into the kinds of animal stories told by Tasmanian Aborigines. The Drogerdy was a rascal of an animal that was nearly killed by a group of hunters and was saved only following the intervention of the great spirit Moihernee. Moihernee was angered that the hunters were harassing the Drogerdy and made them feel so guilty that one of the men crawled into the burrow until he found the beast asleep in its nest. When the hunter tried to pull it out by its tail he discovered it had no tail (in fact wombats do have a tail that is so tiny it hardly seems worth having). Later, when the Drogerdy was finally coaxed out, the hunters begged for forgiveness and said that from now on it would be named Publedina—the digger with no tail. From

NOUVELLE - HOLLANDE : Île King.

LE WOMBAT. *(Phascolomis Wombat N.*

Europeans struggled to describe and draw Australian animals. This beautiful illustration, made by artist Charles Alexandre Lesueur during Francois Péron's visit to King Island in 1802, portrays 'Le Wombat' with many young, yet even twins are extremely rare.

Georges Cuvier's Le Règne Animal, *published in Paris in the early nineteenth century, illustrated what modern palaeontologists have now established as fact: koalas and wombats are descended from a common ancestor.*

2.ᵃ 2.ᵇ

1.ᵃ 1.ᵇ 1.ᶜ

2.

B. Fournier sc.

1 . LE KOALA . Cuv.

(Lipurus . Goldf . Phascolarctos . Blainv)

2 . LE WOMBAT .

(Phascolomys . Geoff)

Wombat carer Gaylene Parker's rule of
thumb is that if a joey's ears are lying
flat on its head or its mouth is still sealed
with a membrane it is too young to raise.
At four months of age this baby's pouch
and tiny tail are clearly visible.

Anyone who takes on the job of caring
for a young wombat should realise that feet,
furniture and flyscreens are all fair game.

Northern hairy-nosed wombats are so rare that this remains the only high-quality photograph of the creature in the wild.

Southern hairy-nosed wombats have a phenomenally low need for water—as little as 22 mLs per kilogram per day. No wonder this one at Taronga Zoo in Sydney looked so unimpressed with the rain.

Koalas and wombats share many characteristics but until Garry Smith and his party of eight skiers in Kosciuszko National Park witnessed this scene in 1995 no-one knew about wombat piggy-backing.

Alan Horsup would love to know what secrets a northern wombat burrow contains. The most basic facts about the subterranean life of this animal remain a mystery.

At Narawntapu National Park you can sit quietly and have a wombat graze almost to your feet.

that moment the Publedina was given the right to dig its tunnels in peace.

A legend from northern Victoria, recorded in the 1950s by the anthropologist Aldo Massola, has it that Koim, the kangaroo, cut off Warreen the wombat's tail during a dispute in which the kangaroo tried to seek shelter in a storm. As the kangaroo fled, Warreen cast a spear into the base of Koim's back. This is why the kangaroo has his stiff upright tail. In a third legend from south-eastern Australia the kangaroo, Mirram, is once again trying to get inside the wombat's shelter, only a more violent altercation breaks out. Mirram smashes a rock into the wombat's head (again Warreen), which is why he has a flat head. Mirram also banished the wombat to live forever in the 'dark, damp hole you call home'.

In a 1970s report to the New South Wales National Parks and Wildlife Service, archaeologist Patricia Vinnicombe said kangaroos, emus and echidnas were often found in Aboriginal deposits along the New South Wales coast but wombats and koalas were not. She notes in her study that young male initiates were prohibited from eating both animals. The avoidance shown in respect to the wombat, a burrowing animal, may have something to do with the fact that in some places, as part of their initiation ceremonies, young Aboriginal men were made to stand with their feet buried; koalas were off limits because they lived so close to the sky god Daramulen.

Barbara Triggs says that possum pelts were worn by Aborigines for warmth and wombat fur was used to make string. Other accounts suggest that wombats and koalas were left alone altogether and never eaten. It would seem logical, though, that just as there are hundreds of names for wombats there may have been hundreds of different ideas about how the creatures should be used or not used. Sadly, like the names and their accompanying stories, much of this knowledge is probably lost forever.

Chapter 4

DANTE GABRIEL ROSSETTI'S PET

The sit is a slightly-excavated area about three square feet and up to ten yards from the entrance of the burrow. It is usually in a sheltered position with a fairly good view. They spend some time sunbaking in the morning and evening and sometimes during a dull day. It is hard to catch them there as they sense your approach, but if you sit quietly or watch through binoculars from some vantage point, you can observe them each morning or evening.

PETER NICHOLSON

Although Bass knew nothing of the Tasmanian oral history about wombats he was nonetheless clearly taken by the beasts he found in Bass Strait. He filled eleven pages with his neat, tight scrawl in his letter that ended up in Sir Joseph Banks' collection. He described the marsupials with an attention to detail and a vividness that provides as good an account of the wombat as has been written in more than two centuries.

I first knew of Bass from a postage stamp I collected in primary school: it was a portrait of him, with his first boat *Tom Thumb* in the background. Tucked under his arm was a spyglass. His chubby face looked friendly and stubborn. A shock of hair was swept off a high forehead. He had a strong nose and a cleft chin. To me he looked to be a man's man. The stamp was part of an explorers set and he had the $2 denomination, which made me think he was the most important. Flinders had the $1 denomination and, because they were friends, I have always kept them side by side in my stamp album. When I was a kid, and even today, this collection has remained one of my most treasured possessions. I would love to have been on the docks in Sydney the day that Flinders and Bass returned from circumnavigating Tasmania; to rummage through their wonders collected from an undisturbed, cool paradise that had been shut off from the world and, of course, to listen to their tales.

It was not until the winter of 2000, however, that I read

young Bass' words. The State Library of New South Wales owns the letter that Bass wrote to Banks and when I obtained a copy I was stunned at how well Bass communicated. His writing whisked me, as if on a time machine, down to Bass Strait on the day that the first European scientist encountered, in the wild, one of the nation's most unusual creatures.

'The wombat is about the size of a turnspit dog,' Bass wrote. 'It is a squat, thick, shortlegged, and rather inactive quadruped with an appearance of great stumpy strength. Its figure and movements, if they do not resemble those of the bear, at least remind one of that animal. All who have seen it have at first sight been sensible of this similarity.'

As he writes, the creature comes to life. 'The head is large and flattish and, when looking the animal full in the face, seems, independent of the ears, to form nearly an equilateral triangle…the hair on the face lies in regular order, as if combed.'

Its eyes, he observed, were quick and lively and the number of teeth in both jaws amounted to twenty-four. He politely pointed out that the wombat has a thick short neck, which 'greatly restrains the motions of the head'. It has a 'curious little tail' invisible except when the hair of its 'hindmost parts' are parted. Stomach, testicles, penis, legs, paws, claws, ears, nose and diet are then described in fine detail. The flesh, he remarked, was 'very palatable'. The meat he ate was light-coloured, tough with an oily greasiness. Flinders was less generous about the wombat's potential for fine dining: 'Its flesh something resembles tough mutton— there is not too much meat upon it for three or four people to eat in a day.'

'On the islands,' Bass continued, 'he feeds during the day, but on the blue mountains where man also resides, he feeds during the night only, as the natives say. And I think it true because I, as well as many others, have been several days together in those mountains in places that abounded with what I have since learned to be wombat dung but at the time took it for dung of the kangaroo, and never saw a wombat.'

Bass was not given a demonstration of the wombat's speed and made some fallacious assumptions. 'Amongst the qualities of the wombat,' he opined, 'he lays no claim to swift-ness of foot; most men could run it down. Its pace is hobbling or shuffling something like the awkward gait of the bear.'

Bass described the noise of a wombat as a 'low cry between a hissing and a whizzing'. This cry, he commented, could not be heard more than thirty-odd metres away and was never emitted except in anger. Others later compared it to the sound of a kangaroo, or marsupials such as quolls. It is in fact one of those animal cries that is both scary and scared in equal parts—a shriek that would make an intruder really think twice about going any further into a burrow. The impression that I got was of a primitive low cry that evolved tens of millions of years ago from some long abandoned member of the family—a smaller ancestor that needed to make a fuss. The wombat, however, is now a big animal and its noise seems like overkill, comparable to the loudest 'ssshhhh' sound that a human can muster. And, as Peter Nicholson discovered, they make another 'huh' or 'hhhmmpphh' sound when communicating with each other.

Then comes the true treat of Bass' account: 'Seeing one feeding on the seashore and not caring to shoot him I approached unperceived to within thirty yards of the inexperienced creature then gave chase. When up with him that he might not be hurt, I snatched him off the ground and laid him along my arm like a child. He made no noise, nor any effort to escape, not even a struggle. His countenance was placid and undisturbed and he seemed as contented as if I had nursed him from his infancy. I carried him for more than a mile and often shifted him from arm to arm and sometimes, to ease my arms laid him upon my shoulders; But he took it all in good part. At last being obliged to secure his legs whilst I went into a copse to cut a new species of wood his anger arose with the binding of the twine, he whizzed with all his might kicked and scratched most furiously and snipped off a piece from the elbow of my jacket with his long grasscutters.

Our friendship was at an end; for although his legs were untied in a few minutes, he still remained implacable and ceased to kick and scratch only when he was exhausted. He was so constantly on the watch to bite that I dare no longer trust him on my shoulder and scarcely upon [my] arm. For two miles to where the boat was lying, he kept up his pranks.'

'The habitation of the wombat is underground both on the islands and in the [Blue] mountains,' Bass concludes. 'He is admirably adapted for burrowing. When pursued he makes directly for his hole, and even if his hinder parts should be caught hold of is extricated with great difficulty. But a charge of powder blown into his hole soon dislodges him. The form of the hole is not known, no-one having laid any of them open.'

On 27 May 1799, Bass once more put pen to paper. This time, Bass signed, dated and addressed the correspondence to Banks. He introduces himself with the air of a young man, proud of his achievements but aware of the bigger world in which Banks was moving. 'I discovered in 39 degrees south a strait which divides Van Diemen's Land from New South Wales,' Bass informed Banks, adding that he hoped to prepare a full scientific description of the wombat when he returned to England.

What I was most struck by when I had finished reading both Hunter's and Bass' accounts was their struggle to

The Secret Life of Wombats

categorise these beasts in European terms. What must it be like to come to a new continent and have no idea about what lives there? Both letters made me think about the first time I saw a wild wombat and the impact that it had on me. I was seventeen and it was the end of 1985. I had just finished school and my uncle, Brad Hungerford, offered to drop me and two friends into an area of forest alongside Yalwal Creek, behind Nowra. It was an hour-long four-wheel-drive journey that included several deep-river crossings and ended at a shady spot beside a clear waterhole. As Brad was about to drive off he brought out a case of beer from his boot and told us to be careful. That night we drank all twenty-four beers between the three of us—it was the first time that I ever got drunk.

We slept beside the open fire and when I woke in the morning not only did I feel crusty and sick but I knew something was looking at me. I rolled over and found myself less than five metres from a big wombat. We stared at each other for perhaps half a minute. I remember feeling the tiniest flash of fear that this was an animal that could do some damage if it were to charge me. I also recall thinking that it looked relatively intelligent—I am sure that it had been watching me for a long time before I had realised that it was around. Even fifteen years later I can still see the concentration that was etched into its big triangular face, the length of its claws and its chunky legs. At each step its thighs wobbled as if it was a weightlifter holding the barbell aloft for the necessary three seconds. It was my first close encounter with a wild native animal. Before my two friends woke up the wombat turned around and disappeared down its hole, its backside filling the tunnel. We camped in that spot for a full week and never saw another sign of the creature.

In 1800 Englishman George Shaw published the first scientific paper on the wombat in his mammoth work, *General Zoology*. In it he gave the animal the common name Ursine Opossum. Its scientific name was *Didelphis ursina*.

'The largest of all the opossums,' Shaw wrote in his landmark book. 'Size of a badger: colour pale yellow: fur longish and sub-erect: nose strongly divided by a furrow. Native of New Holland: a species very lately discovered, and not yet fully or satisfactorily known or described.'

During one lunch hour I walked from my office across to the Australian Museum where a first edition of Shaw's work is held as a prized possession. It was laid out on a pillow before me and I was able to turn its pages and see the first strange drawings of wombats by Europeans. It is hard to believe that only 200 years ago wombats were a total mystery.

In 1802 the wombat trail took another strange twist. The French, led by Nicolas Baudin, were in Sydney recuperating from their difficult travels around Australia and were the subject of much conjecture by Sydneysiders as to what their intentions were.

On 18 November the two French ships, *Le Géographe* and *Le Naturaliste*, accompanied by a locally built boat purchased by Baudin and named the *Casuarina*, left Port Jackson after nearly half a year of rest and reprovisioning. On 20 November Baudin was off the south coast of New South Wales and was hailed by a passing schooner, skippered by a captain whom the French had met while in Van Diemen's Land. On board was a large wombat that the skipper had collected for Baudin following a request to keep anything interesting he might find. An undoubtedly terrified wombat was then transferred from the schooner into the hands of the scientists. On 7 December the Baudin expedition arrived at King Island. There fishermen sold the French more animals including dwarf emus, a tame kangaroo and several wombats, all of which arrived safely in France on 24 March 1804.

The British were also helping themselves to native animals. Mr Brown, the 'eminent botanist' who had travelled with Flinders, returned to England with a wombat taken from the Bass Strait islands. Upon arrival in the United Kingdom it lived for two years as a domestic pet in the house of a Mr Clift of the Royal College of Surgeons. Ellis Troughton, author of the twentieth century's most enduring text on the continent's mammals, *Furred Animals of Australia*, wrote of this wombat's good fortune. 'Many famous anatomists of the day made its acquaintance, including Everard Home, who observed [in 1808] that it burrowed at every opportunity, was very quiet in the day and active during the night. It ate all kinds of vegetables, but was particularly fond of new hay which was eaten stalk by stalk, taken into the mouth like a beaver, in small bits at a time. It was not wanting in intelligence, and appeared attached to those who were kind to it, putting its fore paws on their knees, and sleeping in their laps if taken up. It good-naturedly allowed children to pull or carry it about, and if it bit them it did not appear to do so severely or in anger.'

Regent's Park Zoo acquired its first wombat, a common, on 26 October 1830 and its first hairy-nosed on 24 July 1862.

Professor Rod Wells, editor of *Wombats*, the marsupials' definitive scientific text, writes that in the nineteenth century wombats attracted enormous public attention but were then displaced by the koala and after a period of time the panda. 'Wombats were kept at Regent's Park Zoo in London in the mid-nineteenth century and indeed bred for the first time in captivity there in 1856. Wombats were favourites of the pre-Raphaelite Rossetti and in the 1860s had developed something of a cult following among his influential friends and family.'

Poet and painter Dante Gabriel Rossetti was an obsessive visitor to the 'wombat's lair' at the zoo. He owned two wombats, which he purchased from an animal dealer for £8. 'Rossetti was the planet round which we revolved,' wrote Val Prinsep, a friend. 'We copied his way of speaking. All beautiful women were stunners with us. Wombats were the most beautiful of God's creatures.'

Wombats in strange contexts began to figure in his drawings and when Rossetti's first wombat died on 6 November 1869 he made a sketch titled, 'Self portrait of the artist weeping at the wombat's tomb'.

Some even credited the animals with supernatural powers. 'The natives state…that it sometimes indulges in a long ramble,' wrote John Gould in 1855, 'and, if a river should cross its course, quietly walks into the water and traverses the bottom of the stream until it reaches the other side.'

Wombat fever reached its peak in 1857, also known as 'the year of the wombat'. One author, Francis Watson, called the creatures 'droll and fubsy'. Here was the beginning of the wombat's reputation as an unwitting comedian. 'Bumbling about on its fat little legs, a poltergeist in Camelot, the rotund and plushy wombat can be allowed to preside over a year of bizarre concatenations of events and characters.'

Back home, though, wombats were being slaughtered as either a pest or food source, but definitely no icon. Wombats

I never reared a young Wombat
To glad me with his pin-hole eye,
But when he most was sweet & fat
And tail-less, he was sure to die!

Rossetti mourns his loss: 'I never reared a young Wombat / To glad me with his pin-hole eye, / But when he most was sweet & fat / And tailless, he was sure to die!'

came to be a highly regarded addition to early colonial menus. 'The meat supply often consisted of roasts of wombat, or "badger" as the bushmen called them,' Troughton writes. 'It was once said that had they been called "wild pigs" they would have soon been eaten out, though fortunately for the vanishing animals the flesh does not resemble pork at all: it is of a musky not very agreeable flavour and very sinewy.'

The Secret Life of Wombats

One by one, however, the populations of wombats that had survived on the Bass Strait islands for nearly ten millennia died out during the nineteenth century due to hunting and habitat change. Each population was subtly different from all the others and the tragedy of their disappearance is that we have no way of appreciating what we have lost because they vanished before they could be properly studied.

In 1802 the crew of the *Cumberland*, a ship sent from Sydney to King Island in Bass Strait caught four dwarf emus (now extinct), three 'badgers', three 'porcupines' and a kangaroo. Some eighty years later, in 1887, the Victorian Field Naturalists Club visited the island and no trace of any wombats could be found. Wombats have become extinct on Preservation and Cape Barren islands and until 1908 it was also thought the Flinders Island wombats were gone. Luckily, though, small remnant populations survived and some of the residents of the island are now dedicated to these wombats' survival. The Bass Strait wombats are attractive animals with long coats, reminiscent of bison writ small. They appear to be as comfortable with the sand and sea as they are with the wind-blasted rolling hills.

On 5 February 1803 George Bass left Sydney in command of the *Venus* for a voyage to South America. He was never heard from again and no trace has ever been found of his ship. He was thirty-two.

Chapter 5

A LOST KINGDOM

The wombat belongs to a very ancient Australian family of marsupials. Fossils of its ancestors are well known: one is the Diprotodon. The wombat family differs from most other marsupials in making burrows underground and in the arrangement of the teeth and some of its bones.

PETER NICHOLSON

In late September 2000 I was sitting in a small aeroplane, at Mount Isa, in outback Queensland, waiting for take-off and feeling like a dog locked in a car in the middle of summer. It was so hot it was hard to breathe. On board in front of me was Dr Philip Currie, one of the world's most famous dinosaur experts, who runs the Dinosaur Provincial Park in Alberta, Canada, and his palaeobotanist wife Eva Koppelhus. Behind me was another well-known fossil expert, Dr Stephan Schaal, the head of research at Messel in Frankfurt, Germany. Messel is a world-heritage listed site whose sediments have yielded remarkable insights into the evolution of animals such as horses. Schaal's team has discovered fossils of mares the size of small dogs, and in the weeks he was in Australia his colleagues were stripping the sediment from one terrier-sized fossil horse with a foal in her womb.

A second plane containing another assortment of eminent fossil experts, including Australia's most famous palaeontologist Professor Mike Archer, was behind ours.

We were heading for the Riversleigh world-heritage fossil site—a precious location 250 kilometres north of Mount Isa. In spite of its scientific importance, Riversleigh's remoteness means that it is in dire need of better management. The Australian scientists are seeking help and advice that could help protect the site, hence this gathering of world-class palaeontologists. The rocks at Riversleigh tell the story of how Australia acquired its exceptionally specialised and evolved marsupials. Although wombats haven't lived there for thousands of years, the bones of their ancestors have been fossilised continuously in this area for more than 25 million years. This includes the biggest wombat that has ever lived—a beast that weighed up to 250 kilograms.

Riversleigh is where the wombat family album is kept. It was first identified as a fossil site at the turn of the twentieth century and then re-worked in the 1960s by an American team who didn't twig to its vast wealth. When Mike Archer arrived in 1976, straight out of university, he realised that he and thousands of other palaeontologists could spend their entire careers there. Around 50 million cubic metres of fossil-bearing rocks are still lying undisturbed at Riversleigh. What has been learned about the evolution of Australia's fauna from the work of Archer and his teams has already revolutionised our understanding of the prehistory of Australia. Yet this rewriting of marsupial evolution has resulted from the collection of a mere twenty cubic metres of rock by the scientists each year since 1976.

Before finally taking off, the pilot of our aeroplane directed our attention to the location of emergency water supplies and rations. Across the country we were heading, such information was not something to ignore—in the heat we were experiencing we would have only a few days to live should we crash without water. Extreme temperatures at that time of year are the result of what locals call the 'build-up'— the gestation period that precedes the onset of monsoonal rains. Thermals spiral invisibly from the ground to the sky, tossing aircraft unforgivingly, as we were to discover as soon as the plane's wheels left the runway. Even at our cruising altitude of 3000 metres I could feel my toes inside my boots slippery with sweat, compounding a woozy sensation caused by the plane's ceaseless wobbles.

Mount Isa fell behind us without a farewell and all of a sudden we were over an incredibly inhospitable landscape. Dry riverbeds snaked across the flatness. The higher up we got, the more these waterways looked like varicose veins on leathery, blemished skin. I recalled the words of the pioneer Dan Carpenter who had crossed the badlands of Nevada in 1850 and wrote: 'This is the poorest and most worthless country that man ever saw—No man that never saw it has any idea what kind of barren, worthless, valueless, damned mean God forsaken country there is…not God forsaken for He never had anything to do with it.'

Out of the haze, a result of widespread burning-off across northern Australia, appeared the Gregory River. From the air the fossil-bearing mesas around the river looked like a complex, layered profiterole cake. Even from an altitude of thousands of metres the land below us was clearly all sand, boulders and prickles—except for the Gregory, whose waters caught a reflection from the sun as we wheeled around in search of a runway.

Philip Currie is a passionate proponent of the argument that birds are a group of dinosaurs that did not become extinct. As we clambered out of the plane, groaning, searching for hats and sheltering in the slice of shade created by the aircraft's wing, kites and other birds hovered and hunted around the airstrip. Currie looked at these birds of prey with an odd intensity—as if he *really was* seeing dinosaurs. Before we had even had time to get our belongings together or take in the surroundings a speck appeared in the sky. There was a faint drone. Soon the roaring full stop turned into a plane, its wings flicking from side to side as the thermals huffed and puffed. It was a dusty, rough airstrip and we all watched in silence as the second plane dropped down through the shimmering heat haze. The moment it touched the ground spirals of dust swept out from under the wings, reminding me of the graceful sweep of an orchestra conductor's arms. When Archer emerged from his plane it looked as though twenty years of care had dropped off his shoulders, as if his life in Sydney as the director of the Australian Museum was a coat that he was able to shrug off when he arrived in this place.

Onto Archer's head went a giant black cowboy hat—the

Mike Archer surveys Riversleigh at dusk—a motherlode of fossils rich enough to fulfil any palaeontologist's fantasies.

dramatic holes in its peak I later learned were the result of Archer's colleague, Henk Godthelp, using it for target practice with a .22 rifle. Archer is tall and handsome in a rangy way. He has an odd accent, since he was transplanted from Australia to the United States as a baby and then returned in his late teens. In Archer's mouth many words sound as though they have gone through a mangle: 'coffee', for example, becomes 'cawwfee', and he gets ribbed about this by those who know him well. I got the impression that not only is

The Secret Life of Wombats

Riversleigh the backbone of Archer's work—he is into his twenty-sixth year of active field work there—but it is also a place where he has fun and tests out ideas.

Night descends on Riversleigh like a big cold flannel, and with the heat gone everyone relaxes. Small groups gather around picnic tables to discuss their finds; there is no better place and no better company to talk about the origins of life. On the first evening, after a few beers and a couple of bourbons, he said, 'We are nothing but specialised fish,' stopping the dinner conversation dead. 'All land vertebrates evolved from fish. We are micro-scaled, air-breathing fish. The lobe fins became digitated. Fish are the most successful animals on the planet because they're us.'

A few drinks and good conversation in the cool of the evening was something to look forward to. For now though, all of us piled into a minibus that would take us to our camp on the Gregory River.

It hadn't rained for six months and the grass was like straw—as close to death as it could get without actually dying. The heat burned my lungs and the trees on the plains looked as though their spirits had been crushed. It was 41 degrees Celsius. If the planet was flat then Riversleigh, I thought, is how such a world would appear underneath—trees that looked more like roots and termite mounds that looked like stalactites gave the landscape a surreal, sterile feel.

A few minutes later we reached camp on the Gregory River: a dozen canvas tents and a cooking–eating area under a giant shadecloth. The front door of my tent was triple-jump distance from the bank of the river and, as fast as decency allowed after greeting the operators of the camp, I stripped into shorts and prepared to throw myself into the water— deep, clear, unpolluted. The Gregory is a waterway filled with life—archer fish (no relation), the occasional barramundi, turtles, file snakes and freshwater crocodiles. Locals believed until relatively recently that saltwater crocodiles also hunted in the Gregory's waters. After assurance from Archer that it was safe, and a quick cost–benefit analysis in my own mind between relief from the heat and being barrel-rolled by a crocodilian, I was swinging a huge arc at the end of a rope, bombing into the river, swimming down so deep in its warm water that when coming back up, in the last few seconds before reaching the surface, I felt the rush of panic at running out of breath.

When I climbed out Archer told me gleefully that in pre- historic times only a fool would have enjoyed the waters of the Gregory. 'These banks were home to ten-metre-long croco- diles, radiocarbon-dated to 25,000 years ago,' he said. From a palaeontologist's perspective 25,000 years is almost last week. Aborigines would almost certainly have encountered those reptiles. 'Some of them were called cleaver-headed crocodiles.'

You may think that the likelihood of such a reptile turning up is negligible, but over the Christmas of 1994–95 just such a thing happened when a visitor to nearby Lawn Hill reported to herpetologist Dr Arthur White that he had seen a strange turtle. The following winter, excited by the description of the reptile, White travelled to Riversleigh and discovered that this turtle was in fact the same one he and Archer had described from Pleistocene fossils located at the site aged between 25,000 and 50,000 years old. Ancestors of the Gulf snapping turtle, as the new beast was christened, would have once had to contend with the cleaver-headed crocodile—a thought that made swimming far below the surface less attractive.

The Gregory River is the reason why Riversleigh is such a special place. Archer told us that he often drank its water while he was swimming. 'It tastes a little like bore water because of its mineral content.' Minerals have been bubbling from the springs and ground-water table of the Riversleigh region for tens of millions of years and slowly, molecule by molecule, they replace the bones of mammals, reptiles and birds. Even today the skulls and the skeletons of modern creatures that make their way into the river are sealed for eternity in its bed. 'There are cow skulls falling into the river today,' Archer says, 'and within a year they are cemented on so securely that they're hard to shift.'

This is why Riversleigh's fossils are both so well preserved and so bountiful. 'About two years ago 32,000 labelled fossils had been removed from here,' Archer told me. This figure is misleading, however, because a single fossil block—labelled as one item—may contain hundreds or even thousands of bones. 'There are twenty-six institutions working on these fossils,' Archer said with a sweep of his arm indicating the almost fathomless depths of the Riversleigh fossil pot. 'Around 1 per cent are in the Queensland Museum and two million per cent would be still out there.'

When I first saw a block of Riversleigh fossil-bearing rock I was amazed at the violence that time and geography had wrought on the bones. While many of the animals are beautifully preserved with skulls intact, others appear to have suffered an horrific accident. And there were so many of them—the slabs were choked with fossils from top to bottom. Each slab was like a pile of X-rays—remove one image of a crumpled animal body and below is another, with another below that.

Because fossilisation at Riversleigh has been under way for so long, scientists are able to watch the evolution of creatures across millions of years. Most fossil sites offer a glimpse into the moment when an organism is preserved by a single catastrophe—floods, mudslides, the deadly poisoning of a lake, the smothering by ash of an ecosystem after an

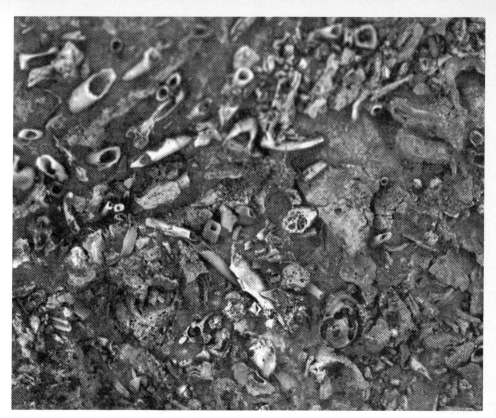

Thousands of fossil bones can be found in a single slab of Riversleigh rock.

eruption. Riversleigh is a long-distance runner in the palaeontological world. For tens of millions of years its mineral-rich
waters have been interring the remains of trillions of animals.

Dromornithids are extinct Australian birds, probably the
biggest avian fauna ever known, and they are preserved in
copious quantities at Riversleigh. Weighing over 400
kilograms and up to three metres tall, they were until recently
commonly named 'thunderbirds'. One of Archer's colleagues,
Dr Walter Boles, dubbed these animals the 'demon ducks of

doom'. Even *their* bones are broken and splintered in ways that, millions of years after whatever disaster befell them, made me wince. And yet right beside a dromornithid's shattered, club-sized drumstick Archer could point out the fingernail-sized jaw of a micro-bat, beautiful in its delicate perfection. On other slabs of rock were skulls that looked as though they had been smashed with a crowbar. Individual teeth were sticking out from stone as if they had been punched free from some creature's face.

These boulders are fractured by light explosives when they are too big to move in one piece and then airlifted back to camp before being freighted in containers for processing in Sydney at the University of New South Wales. Each skull can take months of intricate work. The researchers recover many entire jaws; a complete skull is a stroke of enormous good fortune; and an entire skeleton is sublime. But in some cases the life and biology of an organism has to be extrapolated from a single tooth. Marsupial teeth, like those of all mammals, tell scientists an enormous amount about what an animal was like—whether it was a carnivore, insectivore, herbivore or omnivore. Every marsupial, ranging from a tearer of flesh to a grazer on corrosive Australian grasses, has specialised teeth evolved for its particular food. And in Riversleigh's rocks it is possible to observe the evolution of Australia's marsupials for a huge portion of the time that the continent has been an island.

Ancestral marsupial moles lived in the region, strange diminutive animals that snuffled and tunnelled through the leaf litter of Riversleigh's ancient rainforests. Currently they survive nowhere else on Earth except in the red sand dunes of central Australia. The mountain pygmy possum, Burramys ('burra', Aboriginal for rock and 'mys', Latin for mouse), is today perched precariously in a few final strongholds high in the Australian Alps. It faces extinction as a result of global warming but Archer finds similar creatures throughout Riversleigh's sediments. He suggests that there should be a controlled release of pygmy possums in the Daintree River rainforests of far north Queensland—an environment similar to that which the pygmy possums enjoyed when they were at Riversleigh.

A carnivorous kangaroo lived at Riversleigh, as did another strange macropod with such odd and large canines it is called 'fangaroo'. Also found were tree-climbing crocodiles and marsupial animals so strange that they defy easy classification—one is so weird that Archer and his team refer to it as 'thingadonta'. Early koalas lived there, alongside ancestors of their closest living relative the wombat.

'All of the key steps in wombat evolution are here,' Archer told me. While there are many rich wombat-fossil localities in places like Lake Eyre in South Australia, and although Riversleigh's wombat record is fragmented, nowhere else on the continent is it possible to find representatives of all the major stages of the animal's evolution from 25 million years ago through to as recently as 50,000 years ago.

Marsupials are divided into nine orders, and it is estimated that in the last 55 million years 455 species of marsupials have evolved in Australia. In the same period Australia has hosted at least eighty-five species of bats. In the last five million years there have been sixty-five species of rodent and one carnivorous placental mammal—the dingo which arrived about 4000 years ago. The single primate to call Australia home—human beings—arrived sometime between 60,000 and 120,000 years ago.

Diprotodontia are regarded as one of the most amazing mammal radiations on Earth. Today ten modern families of Diprotodontians survive and, because, typically, living families total only a third of the extinct, scientists assume that during their tenure on the planet around thirty families have evolved in this order. Primates by comparison have had twenty-seven families, and only rodents, with around fifty families, surpass the Diprotodontians for diversity. The order is probably also the most ecologically diverse group of mammals to have existed.

In a recent scientific paper, Mike Archer and his colleague Ken Aplin, curator of reptiles at the Western Australian Museum, point out that of all animal orders only

Diprotodontia includes all of the following: large predatory carnivores (the marsupial lions), specialised browsers and grazers (wombats, kangaroos), leaf-eaters (koalas) and fruit-eaters (brush-tailed possums), insectivores (long-tailed pygmy possum of far north Queensland), nectivores (honey possums and feathertail gliders), consumers of eucalypt sap (yellow-bellied and mahogany gliders), moth-eaters (mountain pygmy possums) and insect-larvae-eaters (striped possums). Members of this order hop, waddle and even fly. They range in size from the fifteen-gram feathertail gliders through to the extinct rhinoceros-sized diprotodon. The only mammal group that comes close to this size differential are the cetaceans—a blue whale weighs more than 4000 times the smallest dolphin. By comparison the biggest Diprotodontian is more than 25,000 times larger than the smallest.

Diprotodontians are broken up into two sub-orders— Vombatiformes (or wombat-shaped things) and the Phalan-gerida (which includes possums and kangaroos). Of the seven types of Vombatiformes, five described families are extinct, three undescribed families are extinct and only two families survive—the wombats and the koalas. By comparison, among the possums and kangaroos only three families are extinct and eight are still with us. According to Archer, while it is likely that both wombat-like creatures and the possum and kangaroo ancestors have been around for at least 35 million years, the

Vombatiformes as a group are—excuse the pun—on their last legs, whereas kangaroos and possums are undergoing an expansion.

One of the most savage and carnivorously engineered mammal predators that has ever lived was a 'wombat-like thing'. *Thylacoleo carnifex*, the marsupial lion, weighed up to 164 kilograms and it shared a common ancestor with the modern wombats. If ever there was a black sheep of *any* family *Thylacoleo* is it. The only mammal carnivore that has come close

The size of Thylacoleo carnifex *is one of the great debates of Australian palaeontology, but would have been irrelevant if it had you by the jugular.*

to it for potential savagery was the 170-kilogram sabre-toothed tiger. Female African lions weigh 130 kilograms and tigers 150 kilograms. Sir Richard Owen first described the species in the middle of the nineteenth century, classifying the Diprotodontian fossil he collected from Wellington Caves in central New South Wales as among the 'fellest and most destructive of predatory beasts'. Steve Wroe, who along with UNSW researcher Anna Gillespie has done much of the work on these fossils, wrote recently that the marsupial lion

Diprotodon optatum *was as big as a rhinoceros, the largest marsupial ever, and prey to both man and beast.*

was a 'muscle-bound, purpose-built ambusher, wrestler and dispatcher of large prey. This beast probably didn't waste time taking out small fry...Pleistocene marsupial lions were extraordinary beasts, distinguished by enormous meat-shearing cheek teeth (carnassials) and built-in flick-blade-like claws on their thumbs. Their meat-butchering carnassials were the largest of any known mammalian predator, living or extinct. In terms of its dentition, many scientists now believe that *T. carnifex* was the most specialised mammalian carnivore of all time.'

Its favourite fare was probably its close relative and the namesake of the family, the giant diprotodon. Some say *T. carnifex* dropped from trees onto its prey, potentially making this distant relation of the wombat's the apocryphal Australian drop bear. From tooth-cut marks scientists have determined that this beast did eat extinct wombats and kangaroos. Humans probably did encounter this marsupial thug—I am imagining the screams of death now—because it is thought they became extinct only 50,000 years ago. It is possible to walk around the Australian outback and see rock paintings done by human beings who may have lived alongside these beasts.

Today there are three species of wombats and a single species of koala. All share one striking physical trait—the heads of their sperm are sickle-shaped. About a dozen species of wombats are known from the fossil record, and they flourished during the great ice ages of the last few million years. Since koalas first evolved 26 million years ago, however, at least eighteen different species have existed in Australia. It may seem then that koalas have undergone a catastrophic collapse in their diversity but this might not be the case—at any time in the last 23 million years there appears to have only ever been a maximum of two species alive. It also seems from the fossil record that at no other time in the palaeontological record have koalas been so abundant in terms of numbers as they are today, although between 26 and 23 million years ago there were eight different species of koala. For only the last 15 million years is there a clear association in the fossil record between koalas and gum trees. No-one can be sure but wombat dentition may have arisen from a long-lost ancestor who was a leaf-eater.

One of the biggest mysteries, however, is how all of these creatures who raise their young in pouches came to be living in Australia in the first place.

Chapter 6

THE FURRY FISH

At Timbertop I was able to assemble a complete skeleton: the teeth are more like a rodent's than a marsupial's and have evolved from its gnawing habits. It has only one pair of upper and lower incisors; none of the teeth have roots. They continue to grow from the base as they are worn down by grinding the roots and grasses which it eats.

PETER NICHOLSON

Three dark ages haunt Australian palaeontologists. During this trio of epochs mammal bones are apparently absent from the continent's stone, denying scientists like Archer a complete account of the evolution of the nation's distinct wildlife. The country's flat terrain, aridity and the lack of 'recent' geological activity sending older layers of sediment close to the surface, have made for an extremely poor fossil record. We might imagine the Australian mammal fossil resource as a 500-page book of which the first 250 are missing. On page 251 a few words remain though they are written in a lost language. The next 125 pages are also absent and then there are another few lines, but at least palaeontologists can decipher meaning from these. After this brief tantalising insight yet another sixty or seventy pages are gone.

Until Archer and his colleagues stumbled across Riversleigh in the mid-1970s, virtually the entire rest of the book was also gone. It is thought Riversleigh's bones were unknown to local Aborigines; they were not included in their legends. The first European to identify the site was the geologist W. E. Cameron who, in 1900, wrote a science paper about bones he had found near Riversleigh Station. They were thought, however, to be less than 2 million years old and of little interest. Archer first decided to head to the site when he heard that a new diprotodon jaw had been found locked in limestone, awaiting retrieval. Almost immediately he and his colleagues realised that they had found a gap that allowed a huge slab of the marsupial history book to be read.

It is in this context that the discoveries there become so important. Without Riversleigh and some of the central Australian fossil sites the national coat of arms would depict two tragic orphans—the kangaroo and the emu—their family history lost. Walter Boles from the Australian Museum has studied the remains of a 25-million-year old dwarf emu from Riversleigh that is very close to the point at which the birds branched off from their close relatives, the cassowaries. The discovery of this primitive bird also tells us something else— the environment may have been beginning to open up. Emus are runners and there is a limit to how much sprinting an animal can do in a dense rainforest. The presence of these early ancestors of modern emus anticipates the gradual slide towards becoming the driest inhabited continent on Earth as long ago as 25 million years.

The first cursed palaeontological dark age in Australia came during the height of the reign of the dinosaurs from 220 million to 115 million years ago. There are jaws from Victoria dated at 115 million years old that are so strange no-one is yet certain where they fit in the realm of furry animals. From Lightning Ridge, an opal mining town on the Queensland–New South Wales border, come a few 100–110 million-year-old fossil crumbs of mammals. Scientists believe that these are monotremes but unlike any of the three living species of egg-laying mammals—platypuses, and long- and short-beaked echidnas—alive today. At that point palaeontologists are plunged back into the darkness again. By the time the light comes on 45 million years later, marsupials and monotremes are both old-timers in Australia, having travelled across the Gondwanan land bridges that once existed between the Americas and Antarctica. This time it is from Murgon in south-east Queensland that scientists gain a glimpse of the evolution of life. Around 55 million years ago marsupials with affinities to South American animals were inhabiting the region, as were distant relatives of bandicoots. And remarkably, terrestrial placental mammals also lived among the marsupials in Australia, while bats haunted night skies.

The oldest placental mammals are 120 million years old—overlapping dinosaurs by at least 55 million years. The oldest marsupials come from North America and are 100 million years old. It may seem as though raising young in a pouch is more primitive than protecting them inside a womb but in fact the opposite is the case. Marsupials are a later evolutionary development than the placental mammals. The reality, Archer told me, was that in a harsh continent such as Australia, 'marsupials have the benefit that they can discard their foetuses at any time'. Placental terrestrial mammals that did once live in Australia appear to have been outcompeted by the marsupials. 'Once the marsupials made their way through South America and into Antarctica their numbers exploded.'

Marsupials give birth to their young when they are essentially still foetuses. The newborn, highly immature baby does most of its developing in a pouch. How unformed a marsupial is at birth can best be understood by the following example: in the case of bandicoots, their young must rely on a completely different jaw mechanism to attach to the teat inside the pouch. All mammals have a hammer and anvil in their middle ear, articulating like a little jaw. This is the remnant of the jaw structure our reptilian ancestors used to open and close their mouths—reptiles in fact still use this primitive anatomical method. Mammals have evolved a totally different jaw but at the time of the birth of a bandicoot it is so immature it must use its reptilian jaws to begin to suckle.

The question of how marsupials outran the placentals in Australia is one of the most important biological questions that can be asked. Why did the placental mammals that so dominated the rest of the world fall by the wayside when forced to compete with Australian marsupials? I put this question to Archer and I could see that the answer is one of the holy grails of his field.

'This is a complex, controversial and to some extent unanswerable question,' he admits. 'In the first place, marsupials are still very common today in South America, and have been for the last 65 million years. In South America they became the bright carnivores (mouse to Kodiak bear in size) that ate the herbivores, which were mostly the placentals. Marsupials also lived in Antarctica until that continent began to freeze over. And they were in Africa, Europe, North America and Asia— the reasons for their declines there about 17 to 15 million years ago are poorly understood although worldwide climate change that occurred about this time is a likely factor. South American marsupials reinvaded North America in the Pleistocene, charging up all the way to Canada to become the American opossum, strong-arming placental competitors out of the way.'

Some suggestions about why marsupials continue to dominate Australia have little or no evidence to support them, he says. These include the kind of cultural-cringe nonsense, taught in schools right through to the 1980s, that marsupials, which were distributed on all continents, are competitively 'inferior' to placentals and survived here only because ground-dwelling placentals failed to reach Australia. 'This appears not to be true,' Archer declares. 'They did reach Australia but marsupials dominated; and marsupials and placentals coexisted in the late Cretaceous of North America but marsupials commonly dominated in terms of diversity.

'More plausible explanations include: chance (maybe there is no explanation for why marsupials dominated South

America and Australia, and placentals the other continents); or, reproductive strategies (marsupials appear to do better than placentals in challenging or unpredictable climates which now and possibly at critical times in the past have characterised Australia); or perhaps part of the explanation is that marsupials can manage their reproductive investment more efficiently than placentals—being able to "abort" their investment at any stage of its development once it is outside attached to the nipple.'

The final dark age from 55 million to 26 million years ago is the most galling for it spans the 30 million years in which many modern families evolved. During this time, life experimented with the concept of marsupialism, but as far as geological explorers such as Archer are able to discern there is no way of knowing what course this evolution took until more fossil sites are found.

During this third dark age Australia became an island drifting northwards from Antarctica at the rate of 100 millimetres a year. Isolation from the rest of the world, global climate change and the local weather-effects wrought by continental drift became the most powerful forces on the direction that life undertook. If we were to travel back to 26 million years ago, when fossil mammal bones again begin to be found, many faces would look strangely familiar. We would also be stunned at the diversity and fecundity of the swampy environment we would find, according to Archer most comparable to the hooting, hyper-colourful rainforests that are found today in Borneo or Brazil. There was then nearly half as much diversity again as there is today in the mega-biodiverse rainforests of far-north Queensland, even though at that time the Riversleigh area was at a similar latitude as Armidale, New South Wales, is today.

During the next 10 million years, from 25 to 15 million years ago, life lived a full-cream existence. Rainforests grew across northern and central Australia and ecological stability fuelled by warmth and abundant water allowed evolution to run riot. It was in this period that the world got to see the first animals that would one day evolve into wombats. The story revealed by digging at Riversleigh is counter-intuitive in some ways—we expect that as time goes by life becomes more and more complex. In fact, in a place like Australia, which has experienced catastrophic climate change, what has survived is a fraction of the diversity which once inhabited this continent. Australia's marsupial explosion was during the early to middle Miocene which ended around 10 million years ago.

'Around 25 million years ago there was an explosion of disparity,' Archer told me, a can of beer in his hand. 'You had a huge range of wildly different things.'

Australia, however, had broken free of Antarctica by about 40 million years ago, 20 million years before the marsupial heyday Archer refers to, and the world was beginning to chill as circumpolar currents began to flow around the south of the planet, preventing the distribution of warm air into Antarctic latitudes. For Australia these ructions in the global weather patterns would eventually mean desertification. 'More than 40 per cent of the families of Australian animals that lived 20 million years ago became extinct,' Archer said. 'The majority of the collapse in diversity was 10 million years ago. That was probably when the last of the great inland rainforests began to disappear.'

Not much is known about the earliest wombat-like creatures. Part of the problem is that wombats, especially the hairy-nosed species, do not often place themselves in situations where they might end up as fossils—they rarely come to water to drink, they don't like building burrows in places subject to flooding, and in the case of the two hairy-nosed species their habitat is semi-arid. What makes a wombat different from all other marsupials and from many other mammals is its jaw. In order to be able to fuel its underground existence a modern wombat has to eat vegetation, such as native grasses and roots, that other animals turn their noses up at. This harsh diet contains high amounts of silicon which would turn most animal teeth to powder. Wombats have overcome this problem by evolving rootless teeth that grow throughout their lives. Most mammals, including humans and kangaroos, have teeth that cling to our jaws throughout our lives, making them extremely difficult to pull out without damaging the bones in which they are held. If our teeth are knocked out or become rotten, they are gone forever. A wombat on the other hand has a remarkable jaw. As I write this I have a wombat jaw on my desk beside my computer. If I turn the jaw upside down the teeth tumble onto my desk. Each tooth looks like a miniature blunt tusk about two and a half centimetres long.

No other dental form of any animal in Australia so beautifully tells the story of how our continent has transformed itself from rainforests to the driest inhabited land on Earth. The reason for this is that the oldest wombat ancestors did not have teeth like this. As the vegetation in Australia deteriorated with the onset of desertifying ice ages and the replacement of forests with grasslands, the crowns of wombat teeth became higher and higher until their roots finally disappeared altogether. Once the roots were gone the teeth could grow continuously, somewhat like our fingernails. Another fascinating aspect of the wombat's bizarre dentition is that the joey's crowns are actually designed for leaf-eating—like those of a koala. While still in the pouch and through a process known as 'thegosis' (tooth-sharpening), the joey's teeth are ground down to a new crown shape appropriate for them to become grass-cutters. The soft, fleshy part of a wombat's mouth also evolved to aid its lifestyle—its lips are very active and, because they are split, a wombat is able to pick the choicest green stems no matter how close they are to the ground.

But these remarkable developments create another problem for palaeontologists—as soon as a wombat starts to chew it wears down its teeth, which makes any analysis of dentition extremely difficult. In a scientific field so dependent on the study of teeth, where the tiniest lump or bump on a tooth means the difference between a carnivore and a herbivore, wombats make a hard task almost impossible. In terms of survival, though, a wombat's teeth are a wonderful tool—if it weren't for its teeth then it would be impossible for such a big herbivore to live in a burrow. It simply could not consume the type of fodder it needs to fuel a tunnelling lifestyle. And a body built for burrowing is the other evolving feature that can be charted through the fossil record. Its massive head, broad powerful hips and sturdy leg bones, combined with an awesome intestinal system, mean that a wombat is very well placed to take advantage of an underground existence. 'If you are underground it's a climate escape, a way of getting out of the heat,' Archer says.

Late on our second afternoon in Riversleigh, Henk Godthelp and Phil Creaser, another of Archer's colleagues, agreed to show me the wombat fossil sites of the area. We began just downstream of camp in a low-lying area of sandy sediments choked with fossilised freshwater mussels which looked so fresh that when I picked a handful up they might have been washed there just months earlier. This was the spot where the chairman of the Riversleigh Society, Arthur White, the man who named the Gulf snapping turtle, also found the jaw of the biggest of all wombats. Its name was *Phascolonus gigas* and alive it probably weighed up to 250 kilograms. This was truly a wombat writ large. It had unrooted teeth and seemingly all of the remarkable burrowing adaptations.

Dr Lyn Dawson, a palaeontologist at the Australian Museum, who studies much younger fossils than those generally found at Riversleigh, showed me a jaw from one of the giant wombats. A modern wombat jaw sits neatly in an adult's palm, whereas a *gigas* jaw filled both my hands. Dr Dawson put the left tibia of the giant wombat into my hand and I felt like Fred Flintstone holding the remains of a dinosaur drumstick. The front incisors of a common wombat are half the width of an ice-cream stick. The teeth of *Phascolonus gigas* are wider than a ruler and look more like branch-loppers than grass-cutters.

Fossils of this giant wombat species have been found

around Australia including right in the centre of the continent. No-one is sure whether *gigas* dug burrows like modern wombats do but, if it did, the tunnels must have been enormous. It is thought that the giant wombats were still alive until around 50,000 years ago so these early Australian peoples must have seen and hunted these prodigious creatures. It is possible that humans even helped to wipe them out.

Godthelp, Creaser and I travelled away from the river and passed the location of one of the best marsupial and bat fossil sites in Australia. It was discovered in 1985 by Godthelp while he was searching for a lost volunteer who had come to Riversleigh to help dig for fossils. This place is now known as Godthelp Hill. A few hundred metres further down the dusty, rough track we passed another significant site, one that still makes the palaeontologists smile. In 1988—Australia's bicentenary year—Archer, Godthelp and a small swarm of volunteers were working at Riversleigh. Along for the field work was a Laotian palaeontologist called Syp, who one night offered to cook a meal of stir-fried chilli yabbies. Syp walked about a kilometre from camp to catch the yabbies from the Gregory River and quickly had a small bucket-load. Just as he was about to head back to camp a group of ringers from the neighbouring cattle station appeared out of the scrub and asked what the foreign fossil man was up to. When he tried to explain, one of the cowboys walked over, reached into the bucket, seized a yabby and bit its head off whole while it was still alive. He chewed a few times and then spat the gritty contents into the bucket. One by one the other ringers did the same until the bucket contained a soup of crunched-up yabby heads. The terrified Laotian returned to camp and relayed the sorry tale to his colleagues. Syp had the last laugh, however. The next day he stumbled across an extraordinary treasure-trove of bat fossils and it was unanimously decided, since the year was 1988, that the new location would be called the 'Bitesantennary site'.

Pressing on past the Bitesantennary site, Creaser, Godthelp and I climbed the Gag Plateau in our four-wheel-drive until we reached the Encore site. The temperature was over 40 degrees Celsius. We left the vehicle and headed for the birthplace of modern wombats. Between 10 and 12 million years ago this spot was sclerophyll forest and the home to the genus *Warendja*, a little wombat—the smallest species of wombat that is known. Its name originates from the Woiwuro Aborigines. These people, who lived near Melbourne, called wombats 'warendj'; the 'a' was added for taxonomic purposes. The animal was probably only half as big again as a brush-tailed possum. Many of its features are strikingly primitive in spite of its slender and diminutive appearance. *Warendja* survived until a few tens of thousands of years ago. It seems to have been a comparatively swift animal, and some scientists argue that it filled a similar ecological niche to the introduced rabbit.

As we got close to Encore, spinifex dug into my shins through my jeans. 'There it is,' said Creaser. Before me was a pile of boulders and a pit from which the *Warendja* fossils—some molars, pre-molars and a jaw with a few teeth—had been extracted. These ancient fossils are at least 5 million years older than the next true wombat fossils. In spite of my discomfort I tried to imagine a grumpy little wombat emerging from his burrow 12 million years ago. What was his world like?

We walked across a plain in the hot sun until we reached a place where boulders were tumbled on top of each other leaving deep dark cracks. This site is called Cleft of Ages and it is the location of yet another crucial point in wombat evolution. From here the fossil remains of a animal called *Rhizophascolonus* were recovered, dated to around 17 million years ago, when life in Australia was still exceptionally wet and balmy. It is very much a wombat-like creature but its teeth have roots and hence are locked into its jaw. *Rhizophascolonus* fossils have also been found in the Simpson Desert.

After a few minutes we climbed back into the four-wheel-drive, and visited several other sites where a zoo's worth of fossilised marsupial species had been found. In camp later that night Archer explained the significance of the *Warendja* and *Rhizophascolonus*.

'*Warendja* is the first time that we see a wombat that has no roots in its teeth,' Archer told me. 'That indicates that for the first time wombats are specialising on eating something abrasive. They needed to have teeth that grew all through their life. Encore is probably the beginning of the modern radiation of wombats.'

From the *Rhizophascolonus* jaws that have been found at Riversleigh and elsewhere, palaeontologists are able to say that from as long ago as 25 million years pre-wombats were beginning to specialise on some abrasive leaves or perhaps branches that other animals could afford only if they were prepared to fork out thousands for a visit to an orthodontist. But what interests scientists is that grasses only became a dominant feature of the Australian landscape in the last 5 million years. This means that when we look back in time and see a fossil wombat like *Warendja* pulled out of Encore, we are seeing a creature with potential unfulfilled. *Warendjas* and other primitive wombats could not have known that Australia was to become a desert but evolution was already making sure that at least some of the marsupials would be ready to take advantage of aridity. Wombats, kangaroos and koalas are the great beneficiaries of the drying of Australia.

As Archer finished talking I suddenly remembered what

he had said earlier about humans being nothing more than micro-scaled, air-breathing fish. 'Mike, if humans are fish then what's a wombat?' I asked.

'A wombat,' said Archer, without a moment's hesitation, 'is a fat, furry fish that likes to dig burrows.'

Chapter 7

WOMBAT FINISHING SCHOOL

The mother wombat usually has only one young, or very rarely two. She suckles her young in a pouch in which it remains until it is fully furred, about mid-November. The mother makes a simple nursery of near-dead bracken fronds and bark at the end of a tunnel. The young wombat learns tunnelling in the mother's burrow and gradually digs its own small burrow inside the mother's. About four months after it leaves the pouch it leaves the burrow and goes in search of a deserted burrow or place to dig its own. Often it meets failure when it digs in a creek bed and the burrow is flooded.

PETER NICHOLSON

Soon after my return from Riversleigh I had a vivid dream. I was in a field of grass on an enormous plain in outback Australia. There was no sign anywhere of other people. It was silent except for the sound of a cold wind. The sky was blue like the sea, and only two other colours were visible as I turned around and took in the strange landscape—the straw-coloured grassland and the brown fur of a group of enormous giant wombats, *Phascolonus gigas*. They were grazing, tearing whole tussocks of grass apart with their teeth with a relentless shearing motion and they were oblivious to me. Their enormous size had me transfixed. They slowly swept up their feed and moved closer, eventually passing me by. That was it. Nothing else happened but I knew I had come as close as I ever would to knowing what *Phascolonus gigas* was like in the wild. The world I saw in my dream was ice-age, inland Australia prior to the arrival of people.

At the time of human settlement there were five genera of wombats compared to the two alive today. Some of these were probably competitors as their territories must have overlapped. There were at least two species of common wombats—an east-coast and a west-coast variety. The west coast's common wombat lived on the extreme south-west tip of Western Australia and may still have been alive a mere 10,000 years ago.

For most Australian wildlife, the horseman of the

apocalypse was climate change. Human hunters and other predators were able to 'mop up' the last specimens of the megafauna that had been made vulnerable to extinction by the changes wrought on their habitat by desertification.

What must it be like to be the last of your kind? I could imagine fates for the last *Phascolonus*—being carved up with stone blades by a group of joyous Aborigines. I could envisage the last little *Warendja* small enough to fall prey to a wedge-tailed eagle. The last *Ramsayia*—another large primitive fossil wombat that likely survived until the arrival of people—may have been as big as *Phascolonus* and I imagine the final individual in this genus dying of old age deep in its burrow, years after its mate succumbed to a terrible ice-age drought.

Eventually, though, *Vombatus* and *Lasiorhinus* were the last wombats standing. It was time for me to find out what these living wombats are like.

A few weeks after I had returned from Riversleigh I drove out to Western Plains Zoo at Dubbo to see their wombat-breeding program. There most of the wombats are not on display—they live in a research facility where veterinarians and scientists are trying to determine how best to breed them. This facility is essentially an artificial warren, allowing researchers the opportunity literally to lift the lid on their subjects at any time. All of the nests are monitored by closed-circuit television and arrays of data loggers are constantly tracking climate variability. In addition, each animal is regularly monitored to assess hormone levels. No wombat has ever successfully reproduced in this environment but chief vet Dr David Blyde is sure that a recipe for wombat breeding is close at hand. A few hours before I arrived, two wombats had been mating and everyone had their fingers crossed for the young couple, which went on to spend the rest of the day biting and hissing at each other. Blyde has supervised procedures resulting in the birth of a black rhino as well as numerous other species of exotic endangered animals, but a baby common wombat has eluded him.

Since my Riversleigh trip with Mike Archer, I was seeing the creatures through the prism of deep time. I could also see how it is that people find them to be such a bewildering-looking animal. Wombats' big leathery noses are like the heel of a callused foot. They have beady little myopic eyes that have a mischievous sparkle and onyx-black depths. Enormous jowls bulk out their thin mouths and they have buckteeth like a beaver. Their heads look like battering rams, capped off by the cutest ears that I have ever seen stuck on any animal's head. They walk as if they have a membrane of skin between all of their limbs, and they have an enormous backside— probably as good an explanation as any why Ruth Park's Muddle-headed Wombat does not wear trousers, only a shirt and a frayed straw hat. I also got the feeling that they were doing some thinking inside their blockheads.

Wombats really do appear to belong to an environ-ment—underground—that we don't understand. Emerging from their burrows they look like tired coal-miners who have no interest in socialising. Wombats seem to suffer life above ground as a necessary evil.

No-one knows anything about the early life of northern hairy-nosed wombats and there is still a great deal to be learned about the southerns. Perhaps as a result of this much of what is known about commons is projected onto southerns and northerns. Several people I spoke to, including Blyde, said the behaviour of young and captive southerns are very similar to commons, with one difference—southerns may be more placid than commons. The common wombat, wrote Ellis Troughton, 'lacks the good-natured twinkle of eye' seen in hairy-nosed species.

'Commons are much more aggressive,' Blyde told me. 'Southerns are much more friendly. Commons just beat up on each other and people—they're really aggressive.' Everyone who works with commons has scars to prove it. Blyde says there is no problem at all keeping southern hairy-nosed wombats together in an enclosure, even a couple of males and a female. 'Commons hate each other.'

Soon after visiting Blyde at Dubbo I travelled to Taronga Zoo to watch as two southern hairy-nosed wombats were

Vombatus ursinus, *the common wombat. This wombat's nose resembles the sole of a* *foot, yet all three species have a split lip, which enables them to pluck even the shortest blade* *of grass.*

moved into a display enclosure together. These wombats had much silkier fur, a distinct silvery-grey colour. Their hairy snouts are longer than those of the commons. Their eyes definitely did not have the psycho, touch-me-if-you-dare look about them that the commons have and there was something almost doleful about the way they looked up when the lid to their box was opened.

To learn about common wombats there is no better place to start than Gaylene and Rob Parker's home at Wingello in the southern highlands of New South Wales. Their property is an hour-and-a-half drive south-west of Sydney, on bushland a short drive from the Hume Highway. Thirty common wombats live there, including seventeen that need bottle-feeding twice a day with a special formula with the brand name 'Wombaroo'. This is made up of whole-milk solids, milk fat, vegetable oils, vitamins and minerals. The Parkers have so many wombats to feed that they purchase Wombaroo in 12.5-kilogram bags. On average, before graduating from what Gaylene calls the 'wombat finishing school', usually at the age of two years, the average orphaned wombat consumes between $100 and $200 worth of formula.

The Parkers are members of a native animal care group known as the Wildlife Information and Rescue Service. When someone finds an injured animal it is to WIRES that they turn. WIRES provides training for those who wish to become wombat carers, but before the responsibility for a joey can be taken on a licence must be obtained from the state's wildlife agency. Wombat young often survive inside the pouch for days after whatever accident claimed their mothers. Gaylene once found a baby wombat inside its mother on a farm—according to the landholder the adult had been dead for nine days. On other occasions the baby wombat will climb out of its dead mother and stay in close proximity until it dies of starvation, is eaten by a predator or rescued by a passer-by. The nearby expressway exacts a frightening toll on marsupials, which are totally unevolved to cope with cars hurtling through the night at speeds well in excess of 110 kilometres per hour. In this area, surrounded by agricultural land, wombats also run foul of farmers, who often regard native animals as an extreme pest. And as Sydney sprawls outwards, greater pressure is applied on landholders to subdivide. Suburbanisation brings more dogs and people, forcing wombats to burrow beneath houses or to find new habitats. This story is being repeated almost everywhere in Australia where wombats survive.

When a live wombat is discovered inside a dead mother a strict protocol is followed that can make the difference between life and death to the young. Tugging it out through a pouch can break its bones, and hauling it off the teat can damage its delicate jaw. The pouch of the mother needs to be cut open and the joey can be removed only after the suction between the mouth and the nipple has been gently broken. Immediately after rescue a joey should never be held close to a human chest: the smell of a person and the sound of a human heartbeat will terrify it. Instead, the Parkers rub a cotton pillow case over the body of the mother to collect her scent, and use this to ferry the baby to safety.

A young wombat's bond with its mother is extraordinarily enduring and intense. It spends most of its first year in the darkness of her pouch with a constant supply of milk produced by two teats. Their milk is rich in immunoglobulins, unlike the milk of placental mammals, which is rich in lactose. The main carbohydrate component of wombat milk has a name more like that of a distant galaxy—oligosaccharides of galactose.

When the mother is in her burrow this darkness must be absolute. The male plays no part whatsoever in wombat-rearing. It was not until 1990 that scientist Clive Marks, using infra-red camera equipment, captured wombat sex in the wild. Until this amazingly patient piece of field work was conducted at Tonimbuk in Victoria it was assumed that wombats copulated in their burrows. With his infra-red equipment Marks had a clear view over ten hectares of common wombat habitat, and in April 1990 he watched a pair get to 'know' each other in the biblical sense.

'The female lay on her stomach while the male lay on his side at right angles to the female,' he wrote. 'Copulation involving rhythmical thrusting by the male occurred over three minutes and twenty-two seconds in the first instance. At the end of this time the female rose from the prone position and immediately broke into a trot, pursued by the male. The female ran in wide circles and figures of eight, periodically slowing and allowing the male to catch up to her. Chasing behaviour extended over two minutes and nine seconds until the male delivered a powerful bite to the hindquarters of the female.'

Then the whole show began again and was repeated on seven occasions over a twenty-five-minute period. No-one has ever seen southern hairy-nosed wombats having sex in the wild, though in captivity copulation is similar to the commons, with two notable differences. 'Instead of biting the female,' writes Marks, 'southern males rake their teeth along the female's back, and both animals lie on their sides.'

No-one has any idea how northerns mate. The males of all three species probably fight over females—I have seen wild wombats in frenzied battles for feeding rights, so the odd tussle over a female must occur. The night Marks saw the common wombats copulating, a second male did appear and tried to seduce the female but the scientist lost track of the new couple when they bolted off together into the forest.

Interestingly, Marks observed the mating game to be highly ritualistic, and spread over a large area—at least half a hectare. Maybe, he suggests, this is why wombats have trouble coupling in captivity.

Studying wombats in the wild is a difficult art because these animals are inordinately sly and fast. Much of what we know about their personalities comes from captive or semi-tame animals. Barbara Triggs, however, has dedicated much of her life to watching them in the wild. 'They are extremely wary,'

she writes. 'Although I found that if I stood absolutely still, downwind, they would be unaware of my presence, following them through the forest undergrowth required much patience and practice, and was often unsuccessful. There is also considerable difficulty in observing social interactions between animals that spend most of their time either alone or deliberately avoiding one another.'

Triggs has collected a wealth of information about wild wombats, including their diet: a wide variety of rushes and native grasses such as spear, tussock and kangaroo and, as a delicacy, the white bases of sword grasses. She has also confirmed the comfort factor of living in a burrow—on three consecutive summer days, in which the air temperature in the shade near her home in east Gippsland reached 39 degrees Celsius, a mere three metres inside the burrow it never exceeded 26.5 degrees. She observed how, late on a summer's day, a wombat would move closer to the entrance of its burrow, probably to get a feel for the temperature. Researchers have found that the seasons influence the amount of time wombats spend outside their burrows. In winter, Triggs discovered, as little as five hours is spent foraging but in summer this can increase to eight hours. On really hot days, however, she learned that a wombat will stay in its burrow until well after midnight or until the temperature has dropped below its comfort threshold of 20 degrees. Triggs also helped disprove the myth that wombats are slow and bumbling—the only time they dawdle, she says, is when they are grazing. Mostly they travel surprisingly large distances in short periods of time. Triggs followed a wombat one evening for four kilometres before the marsupial shook off the researcher. Nicholson and many others attest to the distances a wombat can move when it is of a mind to travel. Gaylene Parker has radio-tracked wombats in excess of five kilometres in a night.

No-one has ever seen a wombat actually being born. Its gestation is less than a month. The jelly-bean-sized baby probably takes only a few minutes to travel from its mother's birth canal to the pouch, a distance of about ten centimetres. If wombats are like other marsupials, that momentous journey is made without any help; the embryo-like creature will reflexively grasp the female's fur with the claws on its front legs. About a month later it weighs around five grams and is seven centimetres long. By three months of age growth has been astonishing and the young wombat weighs 250 grams; at four months it has reached 400 grams and its eyes are open. Fur begins to appear a month later. At six months the baby has teeth and can grasp the occasional blade of grass from the safety of the pouch.

'No actual observations of the mother cleaning the young in the pouch, or attending to it in any way, have been recorded,' says Barbara Triggs in *The Wombat.* 'It is not known how the young wombat copes with its waste products, but it seems likely that the mother licks the cloaca of the young when it is very small, to remove urine and faeces in the same way as a kangaroo mother does, although it is anatomically much more difficult for a wombat to reach its head into the pouch.' As a general rule, researchers find wombat pouches to be surprisingly dirty.

By seven months the wombat weighs two kilograms and is moving in and out of the pouch. Between eight and ten months it is able to leave the pouch permanently, and between twelve and fifteen months the wombat is weaned—sometimes only after stern treatment from its mother. Yet the bond between the two remains close even after weaning.

At two years of age it is time for the twenty-two-kilogram marsupial to make its way in the world. No-one knows how long a common wombat can live in the wild. Captive animals have lived as long as twenty-six years. Barbara Triggs suggests their life expectancy is about fifteen years. When a human baby is born it weighs an average of between three and four kilograms and by the time it is an adult will have increased in weight about twenty times. When a wombat is born it weighs a gram and may grow by 30,000 times to reach its peak.

The smallest wombat that Gaylene Parker has ever cared for weighed a mere 113 grams—the weight of two average-sized eggs. At that age a wombat is completely hairless and needs to be moisturised twice daily with Sorbolene cream in order to prevent its skin cracking and bleeding. This lubrication is normally the job of the mysterious pouch. Preliminary studies by Professor Russell Baudinette of the University of Adelaide suggest that pouch fluid consists of two main substances: antigluing lipids that stop the joey from getting stuck and keeps its skin moisturised and peptides that kill bacteria. An animal of this size is so hard to raise and involves such a long-term commitment that WIRES generally recommends that wombats rescued before they are 110 days old be put down.

WIRES also advises that all hand-reared wombats be raised in pairs. 'Most joeys raised singly will learn to climb into human beds and will suck holes in sheets, doona covers and night dresses,' says the organisation's guide to raising wombats. 'Eventually tired and distressed they find their way to the coolest part of the house, knock over the linen basket and hiccough themselves amongst the "mother's" soiled underwear. This behaviour is not unlike that of a small child crying itself to sleep and sucking its thumb. Joeys raised in pairs show none of these symptoms...Two young wombats can be introduced to one another by hanging separate pouches fairly close together. The first few encounters can be argumentative, but within a day or so you will find both joeys curled up happily together in one pouch.'

This pairing means that the Parkers have the equivalent of eight sets of twins. Soon Gaylene and I were heading out into the enclosures dotted around their property to begin the enormous task of feeding.

'They don't answer to their names,' Gaylene declared as we approached the first enclosure. 'It doesn't matter what you call them—at this age they always come running.'

Even so, every wombat has a name and to coax the animals out of their burrows Gaylene makes a 'ssshhh' sound and gently calls them. The first pair was soon spotted. She sat on the ground and held one wombat in her arms while the other put its paws up on her legs. Each wombat had its own bottle of warm formula and they appeared to be in paradise while they were drinking. I was reminded of a comment in a book on the wombat's relative called *The Koala*. Its authors, Roger Martin and Katherine Handasyde, said people were so in love with koalas because their head-to-body ratio is 1:3— similar in size and posture to an eighteen-month-old infant. I realised then that these quiet moments with her 'babies' must be what helps make Gaylene's task so rewarding. She even let a few drops from the bottle trickle onto her skin on the inside of her wrist to check the temperature—exactly as a parent would do for a human baby. The whole time she was feeding she preened the wombat's fur, looking for ticks or irregularities.

'They nearly always have their eyes closed while they feed,' Gaylene said as I held the bottle in place for the wombat which fed while it was standing. Its fur was very different from its companion's and I was struck by how distinctive each of the Parker wombats are. Barbara Triggs noted this variety too. 'Glossy black, dark grey, silver-grey, chocolate brown, grey-brown, sandy and cream-coloured wombats are all

Gaylene Parker's wombats are fed in pairs but take it in turns being in her lap or standing while they guzzle from their bottles.

found,' Triggs writes in her book. 'A small colony of ash-white wombats, with dark eyes and pale yellow markings on the face, is found on Wilsons Promontory in southern Victoria.' I remembered Peter Nicholson's albino.

Another difference that Gaylene pointed out to me was in their whiskers. One animal had perfect sets of whiskers that looked as though they were groomed straight—long whiskers on either side of its sensitive but tough-looking nose. A second had frizzy, messy whiskers. A wombat actually has five sets of whiskers. Apart from the biggest there is also one set above the eyes, another on the cheeks, a set under the chin and yet another near the throat.

At the next enclosure I was handed a baby called Badger which sat in my lap and took the teat into its tiny mouth. My hands were under its chin and I could feel how immensely solid the jawbone was, like a triangle of steel inserted under the skin. Badger had a musty, dusty odour. When he had finished feeding he threw his head back and waited for me to give him a scratch.

'You need to scratch harder than that,' Gaylene said, 'Wombats are such full-on animals that if you do things too tentatively they get scared.'

The next two pairs of wombats on the feeding schedule had not yet graduated to burrows and were inside their pouches in a little shed. The homemade pouches are old army canvas bags into which jumpers, arms and neck sewn up, and a pillow case are placed. The two animals were brought inside the house for their bottles. When Ticky emerged from his bag his energy was extraordinary. He charged around biting, pushing, tumbling and jumping. He was not much bigger than a shoe but he had sharp teeth and a crazy look in his eyes. Gaylene knocked on his skull with her knuckles to demonstrate how hard his head was. It sounded like she was rapping on a log, and Ticky didn't even bat an eyelid. His foot pads, which had yet to experience dirt and digging, were soft. Once he graduates to a pen where he can burrow, the undersides of his feet will become very tough. While he was out of his bag I noticed the entire Parker family raised their feet from the floor up onto the couch. 'There's no malice in him though,' Gaylene said to reassure me. Soon he had me dancing around the lounge room trying to avoid his crash tackles. One of the often-quoted facts about common wombats is that at two years of age their personalities suddenly change and they become hostile even if they were the sweetest of babes in arms.

'This is not true,' Gaylene said. 'They don't change, they just get bigger.'

The Parkers have found that as a last resort the best way to discipline a baby wombat is to give it a nip on the ears. Rob discovered this when one day his hands were full as he was trying to hold a fractious wombat. He gave it a bite on its ear, after which the joey gave a squeal and proceeded to behave itself superbly.

When baby wombats are stressed they hiccough. Chronic stress is made manifest in their claws, which take on a striated appearance. Gaylene says wombat carers need to know one important fact about the animal's eating habits: 'Whatever happens at the head end can take up to fourteen days to show up at the rear end.'

A wombat's constitution allows it to live on almost nothing. Their metabolisms defy easy explanation. One of Australia's great mammalogists, Tim Flannery, told me that he 'can't understand' how wombats work. 'I still haven't been able to put together how they are doing business and it is an enigma how they are able to sustain themselves. They should be part of Australia's economic future because in parts of Australia there would be no better converter of grass to meat. They're three times more efficient at this than kangaroos which is really saying something.' But no-one has as yet attempted to farm them.

Ian Hume and Perry Barboza, researchers in marsupial nutrition, have done the most scientific work to unravel the mysteries of the wombat's digestive system. Its gut capacity is a third greater than herbivores of a similar size and allows for the slow fermentation of fibre. Unlike sheep, kangaroos and cattle, wombats use fermentation as a second step in their digestive process. The easy starches and proteins are absorbed by the stomach and small intestine first before the remaining food is packed off to bacteria that ferment vegetation, extracting every drop of energy. This process can take several weeks.

Urea, a urine waste product that is normally excreted by most animals, is fermented in wombats, allowing them to recycle up to 42 per cent of its nitrogen. Where life is marginal, such abilities give wombats an edge. Wombats also have smaller metabolic organs, such as heart and liver, than other animals their size. A study of southern hairy-nosed wombats has shown that their kidneys are able to produce extremely concentrated urine, which means minimal water loss.

Carers such as the Parkers pride themselves on keeping their charges as undisturbed as possible, attempting to mimic the developmental stages they would undergo in the wild. As soon as the wombats at Wingello are old enough, eight to ten months, they graduate from their fake pouches to enclosures where they are able to dig their own burrows and create their own nests. Ticky would soon have his own enclosure. Aggressive behaviour in a wombat makes Gaylene happy because it is a sure sign the animal will make the transition to the wild.

More than 200 orphaned juvenile wombats have come through the Parkers' home over a twenty-year period—the most on bottles at any one time was twenty-three—and the majority have been successfully rehabilitated. When a wombat is ready for release the door to its pen is left open and it is free to wander off into the state forest and national park that adjoins the Parkers' rear boundary. If a wombat has been successfully rehabilitated it will come and go between its enclosure and the forest for a few weeks before eventually striking off on its own.

This morning, though, four hours had passed and we were only halfway though the feeding program. Normally it takes Gaylene about an hour and a half to feed all of her animals. The whole process would be repeated later that afternoon, and at any time of the day or night Gaylene is on call to head out and attend a rescue, anywhere within her allotted 2700 square kilometres. Without people such as the Parkers, baby wombats may face horrible and slow deaths. The collision between civilisation and the Australian bush can guarantee only that the workload of wildlife carers is certain to increase. Our animals are becoming refugees even before we have begun to understand them.

Life may be tough for the common wombats, dodging cars on freeways, furious farmers in the fields, and mange, but it's nothing compared to the problems their cousins from the north are facing. It was to Queensland that I had to travel next in order to meet the wildest and rarest wombat species— one of the most desperately endangered animals on Earth.

Chapter 8

YAMINON

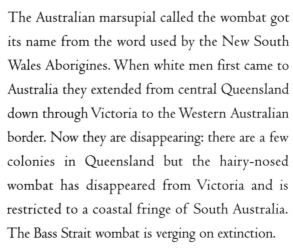

The Australian marsupial called the wombat got its name from the word used by the New South Wales Aborigines. When white men first came to Australia they extended from central Queensland down through Victoria to the Western Australian border. Now they are disappearing: there are a few colonies in Queensland but the hairy-nosed wombat has disappeared from Victoria and is restricted to a coastal fringe of South Australia. The Bass Strait wombat is verging on extinction.

PETER NICHOLSON

In aerial photographs, Epping Forest National Park in central Queensland—about a thousand kilometres south-east of Riversleigh—is shaped like a vandalised hexagon. That state, where up to 450,000 hectares of scrub and forest is removed each year, has the highest rate of land-clearing in Australia. Agriculture pounds against the boundary of the 3300-hectare park and entering its gates I immediately understood why northern hairy-nosed wombats—their estimated population is around a hundred individuals—are in such trouble. The world has run out of space for them and few people seem to care.

By comparison, a thousand wild giant pandas live in China's bamboo forests and they are a mammalian cause célèbre. Zoos clamber over each other to have one on display and the birth of a panda anywhere in captivity attracts breathless media attention. Not one single northern hairy-nosed wombat is in the relative safety of captivity, no-one knows how to get them to breed, they refuse to eat choice pickings of food left for them in times of drought and 90 per cent of their lives is profoundly secret, conducted in giant, complex burrows. To see a northern hairy-nosed wombat at Epping Forest is a rare privilege and one that only a few dozen people have had.

Epping Forest is surrounded by thousands of square kilometres of environmentally degraded rangelands no longer able to support specialised wildlife such as the hairy-nosed wombats. Because of their specific habitat needs, they inhabit only 300 hectares. And this minute habitat is being overrun by a noxious African weed, called buffel grass. Unfortunately for the wombats, buffel is the preferred pasture of the local graziers because it outcompetes native grasses in all variables and is actively seeded throughout Queensland. The wombats appear to construct their burrows only in the sandy soil on either side of an ancient, dry creek bed that bisects the national park. The presence of the tropical bauhinia tree also seems to be crucial for the long-term survival of a burrow—a plant unlike the eucalypt vegetation that covers most of Australia. Scientists speculate that these large trees provide shade that helps modify burrow temperatures and that their roots act like struts in a mine shaft to minimise tunnel collapses.

In spite of being listed by the International Union for the Conservation of Nature as critically endangered, for most locals the wombats are less of a priority than the introduced cattle on neighbouring farms. It is thought that cattle grazing in Queensland is what got the northerns into trouble in the first place but those who manage the park still have to tread carefully when it comes to protecting the wombats. Government officials do not allow feral animal baiting to occur within 500 metres *inside* the southern boundary of the park because they are afraid of killing pastoralists' dogs. And although cattle have been banned from the park since 1981, there are still incursions. The nearest park ranger is three hours' drive from Epping.

In the winter of 2000, 10 per cent of the world's entire population of northern hairy-nosed wombats was eaten by dingoes. On the weekend before I travelled to Epping Forest a conservation team met at Western Plains Zoo and decided the only hope for the wombats is to consider locking them away from the outside world with a predator-proof fence. The price to be paid would be that the population would cease to be wild, but it is not clear where the money to build such a fence would come from. Queensland Parks and Wildlife Service researcher Dr Alan Horsup says he is now effectively 'farming wombats'. Horsup travels to the park several times a year to make sure nothing catastrophic occurs to the population; he oversees all research on the animals and chairs the committee of officials and scientists responsible for them.

Just over a hundred years ago northern hairy-nosed wombats had a range that sprawled across the three eastern states— New South Wales, Queensland and Victoria. It was not until 1983 that scientists put the last pieces of their historical puzzle together. In 1872 Sir Richard Owen, a steadfast and noisy opponent of Charles Darwin's theory of evolution, was the first European to describe a northern hairy-nosed wombat—a fossil skull from the Wellington Caves in central New South Wales. He called the animals *Lasiorhinus krefftii* to honour mammalian palaeontologist Johann Krefft. In 1900 some unfossilised wombat skulls were sent to the Queensland Museum by a Mr Gillespie of St George in south-western Queensland. The new skulls were given the scientific name *Phascolomys gillespiei*. In 1937 two brothers, Charles and Greensill Barnard, were sent to the centre of the state by the Queensland Museum to confirm reports of a 'new kind of wombat'. The pair shot a wombat and sent its skin to the museum where it was named as a sub-species of southern hairy-nosed wombats.

On 2 October 1937, in a letter now held at the Queensland Museum, Charles Barnard wrote: 'My brother and I returned yesterday from another wombat hunt. After a round trip of nearly 800 miles I regret to say that we were unsuccessful in obtaining any more specimens of wombat. We spent a whole week at the place where we secured the first one &, although we kept going night and day, & having traps out, we did not see even one & had come to the conclusion that there were very few animals in the area. There might be 100 burrows in a distance of two miles by half-mile, but from the tracks there might be only 20 animals.'

In 1983 Dr Lyn Dawson set to work trying to untangle the last 150 years of wombat fossil taxonomy on finds from the Wellington Caves. She discovered that the Pleistocene fossil skulls described by Owen, the skulls found by Gillespie, the skins found by the Barnard brothers and the living beast were all the same thing. The northern hairy-nosed wombat is a genuine living fossil, a creature discovered only after it was thought to be extinct.

I have seen fossil northern hairy-nosed wombats at Lake Mungo in New South Wales, where fragments of their skeletons can be found emerging from the eroding dunes. Even more amazingly their burrows too are visible as fossils—metre-wide discolourations snaking across the sand. Alongside the remains of the wombats are preserved skeletons of Tasmanian tigers, perhaps the ancient predators of these animals.

I arranged to meet Alan Horsup at Epping Forest in October 2000 and in the week leading up to my visit he e-mailed me detailed instructions on how we would find each other at night in the middle of this arid outback region. It is such a remote location that Horsup has to have a complicated contingency plan in case visitors do not arrive by a set time. He powers up his solar-charged satellite phone and checks with his wife, Christine, and his office whether any messages have been left; if not he alerts the police and begins a search through the district.

After a three-and-a-half-hour drive north-west of Emerald, including nearly 125 kilometres on dirt road, mostly in the dark, I finally reached a series of farm gates that Alan had drawn on his rough map. In spite of the kangaroos and cattle freely roaming the track I had been forced to travel faster than I wanted because my deadline for arrival was 7.30 and I was running out of time. At 7.25 p.m. I knew I was close but felt on the brink of becoming lost. I retraced my route for a few kilometres before taking a punt on a side track. I crossed a sandy creek bed, which my car slid and struggled through, before reaching a sign warning that Epping Forest could be entered only with a permit. Alan had organised permission for me to spend up to three nights in the forest so I was authorised to drive through the last gate. A few hundred metres past the sign I could see the glow of a campfire and muttered a grateful expletive to myself. It was 7.35 p.m.

When I walked up to Alan to shake his hand he looked as relieved at my safe arrival as I was. He was in the forest with a Green Corps team, a group of young adults aged seventeen to twenty-one are paid a minimum wage to be trained in environmental work and had been sent to the site for a fortnight to help Horsup. In a decade he has not yet had to take his contingency plan further than ringing Christine. Miraculously the worst medical disaster he has had to deal with is an overnight drive from the national park to Mackay on the coast when a researcher's ear was visited by a beetle while he was surveying burrows. As Alan recounted this story it crossed my mind that I would prefer to be lost than to have a terrified insect clinging to my eardrum.

Horsup is a tall and lean New Zealander whose doctoral studies were on rock wallabies. He immediately struck me as having a disarming resemblance to the amiable character BJ in the television series 'M*A*S*H'. He is so like Hawkeye's partner in crime that every time he went inside the camp kitchen at Epping Forest I expected him to return with a home-brewed martini. He came to science via the air force, where he was training to be a pilot. Years in the bush have transformed him into a formidable hand with a campfire, and a plate of stir-fry was awaiting my arrival. He had also warned me that in the heat here, 'the first beer would not even touch the sides'. Then he gave me the bad news. 'They will go extinct within a hundred years if we don't do something,' he said as I started in on the stir-fry and he slotted a beer into a stubby-holder. Considering that season's predation such a prediction seemed to me to be almost starry-eyed. 'The biggest problem for these animals is their name,' he continued.

'They need a single name like the Aboriginal word for the wombats—yaminon.'

I hadn't heard of this word before and, like almost everything to do with the northern wombats, its origins are obscure. It is mentioned briefly in early textbooks such as Troughton's that Gillespie was told by Aborigines that the wombat was known as 'yaminon'. No-one knows for sure what they would have been called—probably, like the commons, there were many names for these creatures in their former vast range. Today, however, 'yaminon' is all that the scientists have to cling to.

By 10 p.m. it had cooled down. Alan decided the hairy-nosed wombats might now be venturing from their burrows. We left camp in his four-wheel-drive. I was perched on the bonnet holding a spotlight powered from the car's battery.

It was a calm night and the wildlife were out in force—almost every sweep of the beam caught the red eyes of kangaroos, bettongs, rabbits and even a tawny frogmouth. For about twenty minutes we drove no faster than ten kilometres per hour along the 'hairy-nosed highway'—a rutted, pot-holed sandy track just wide enough for one vehicle. We did not see even a trace of a wombat.

'You have just driven through the entire range of the northern hairy-nosed wombat,' I heard Horsup declare in a voice muffled by the windscreen. 'There's no point retracing our route. They scare easily and I have never seen one when I have backtracked.'

We drove down some offshoot tracks and into an area where there were only scattered burrows. Nothing.

When we returned to camp the Green Corps team was asleep. Horsup warned that we would be awake between four and five the next morning. He was true to his word and, as the loudest bird chorus that I had ever heard broke out, I could also hear Horsup preparing our breakfast. It would take another half an hour to rouse the last of the teenagers. But by 6.30 everybody was working at a wombat colony a few kilometres from camp.

Once the Green Corps team began their morning of weeding and removing old fences Horsup and I left to survey all 208 numbered burrows. We drove to Burrow 28 where on his last trip the previous month he had found three wombat carcasses showing evidence of being attacked and killed by dingoes. Altogether on that trip in early September he had found five dead wombats. On the day of my arrival he had found another two—one complete mauled body and, a few hundred metres away, a decomposing wombat intestine. Assuming that not all of the dead wombats had been located he estimated that up to ten wombats may have been killed in the previous twelve months.

'If 10 per cent of the world's giant pandas had died in a

year there would be an absolute uproar,' Horsup grumbled. 'I look at burrows differently since we have had this predation problem. Some of these burrows are a bit like a morgue.'

There was no sign of life at Burrow 28. On the chart stuck to his clipboard Horsup made a note: 'No recent activity.'

One of the few ways in which Horsup and his team have been able to obtain any information about the wombats is to trap them—a process which has highlighted how difficult these animals are to study. Unlike most other Australian animals, which are attracted by baits placed in traps, northerns treat any efforts to entice them into a cage with suspicion. The only way the Queenslanders can catch them is to fence off every active burrow system and place traps at exit points in the fences. Then it is a game of patience, while the scientists wait for the animals to succumb to hunger. It takes on average seven nights of being locked inside its burrow for a northern hairy-nosed wombat to choose to walk into a trap. Horsup once waited twelve nights, just hours shy of the amount of time the animal-ethics committee he reports to allowed for the cages to remain in place. When trapping is under way a veterinarian is constantly on-site and the shutting of a trap triggers a radio signal relayed back to a permanently stationed member of the team—a procedure meant to ensure that none of the wombats spends more than one hour inside its cage before it is collected, weighed, tagged and has a blood sample taken before release. Each captured animal gets scored on a scale of zero to five, with zero being dead and five obese. The highest score ever given is four, an extremely healthy specimen.

One animal, known as Male 25, proved to be trap-happy—he was caught fifty-eight times and became the only wombat in ten years for whom Horsup has been able to develop any affinity. Male 25 became the central character in a book called *The Wombat Who Talked to the Stars*, written and illustrated by Jill Morris, who was fascinated by the plight of the northerns.

'When I was studying rock wallabies,' Horsup told me, 'I watched those things every dawn and dusk and I really had a feel for all of their characters. I had names for them, they had quirks in their appearance and personality. But with these wombats it's hard to build up empathy because you don't see the individuals. They are extremely nocturnal, they burrow, their habitat is thickly wooded and heavily grassed and they are very secretive. I hesitate to say this but it is almost as though the attitude they have is that they don't want any help.'

Horsup has tried to catch the entire colony twice and the results have been hugely depressing. Each time forty-one animals were caught. In 1993 the breakdown of males to females was twenty-five to sixteen. In 1999 the sex ratio had worsened—twenty-eight males to thirteen females. Of the approximate hundred northerns alive today, only about 30 per cent are thought to be female. Such a skewed ratio had not been found in trapping efforts by other scientists working at Epping Forest in the 1980s—even when the total population sank to its estimated nadir of twenty-five wombats in 1981. The low number of females may accelerate the deterioration of the northerns' gene pool. With as few as twenty possible mothers, inbreeding and loss of variation are almost inevitable. Already it appears the wombats are beginning a deeply disturbing genetic decline. They have only 41 per cent of the genetic variation that would be found in a population of their closest relatives, southern hairy-nosed wombats. In other words 59 per cent of their variability has been lost. It was in the 1880s that large numbers of cattle arrived in the Clermont district and since 1920, when other colonies in the district became extinct, these northerns have had no opportunities for gene in-flows.

Dr Andrea Taylor, a geneticist at the school of biological sciences at Monash University, has worked on the northern's DNA, relying on blood samples collected during this trapping work. Through her discipline, new insight has been gained into the northern's genetic journey during the last century. Knowing the loss of variability compared to their closest relatives, Taylor is able to calculate the lowest level of the breeding population and suggests that in the early 1980s the sexually active population may have fallen as low as seven to ten individuals. Competition with cattle and the destruction of habitat, combined with drought, has already taken the species to the brink of extinction.

Most interestingly, she obtained DNA from the skins of northern hairy-nosed wombats from Deniliquin, more than 2000 kilometres to the south. These skins were obtained in 1884. The last confirmed sightings of wombats in that location was 1910, though their burrows may have been populated as recently as the 1980s. Not only could she confirm that the two groups were the same species but also that the Deniliquin wombats had significantly more genetic variability than those in the Epping Forest. Taylor and her colleagues also found that a genetic chasm exists between wombats and koalas, with a full 20 per cent difference in parts of their genetic code. As Archer has discovered in the fossil record, this indicates that they have been on different forks of the family tree for tens of millions of years. Taylor also compared this rare species with common wombats. Northerns are between 7 and 9 per cent different from the commons, indicating four or five million years of separation. The southerns and northerns, she thinks, diverged around 1.7 million years ago.

Another interesting result was that two of the common

The northern hairy-nosed wombat, Lasiorhinus krefftii, *has a bigger, flatter snout than the southern. It has black patches around its eyes and, with lengths of up to 1.3 metres, is the biggest of the three species.*

wombats sampled had massively different genetic codes—almost half what is needed to be classified as a different species. This indicates that commons may be slowly speciating—not such a surprise considering their wide range of habitats. We humans share 99.5 per cent of our genetic code with chimpanzees—all of which helps show just how different the wombat species are from each other.

A loss of variability, however, does not always lead to extinction. If 100 separate mouse colonies were allowed to become inbred, Taylor says, ninety-nine would become extinct but the odds are that one would survive. No-one is quite sure why this is so but it means that freak examples exist of stunningly inbred animals living perfectly healthy lives. Perhaps the Epping Forest wombats are that one out of a hundred.

The history of life on Earth tells us that only the simplest of multicell organisms seem able to evade extinction over billions of years. One day, it is certain, we too will be a species at risk. When our time comes for extinction what tricks will our genome play to buy us more time?

Horsup's trapping program has confirmed that the northerns are a long-lived species—six of those caught in 1999 were in excess of seventeen years of age. Only once has a northern hairy-nosed wombat been kept in captivity. Its name was Joan. She was captured in 1966 when cattle farmers neighbouring the park bulldozed a burrow in search of a pet wombat. At that time such an action was neither illegal nor unusual. When she was caught she was already an adult, at least two years old. She lived in a cage with a concrete floor until 1991 when the Queensland parks service required Joan's keepers to give her some sand so she could dig. She died in 1993. Joan's life in captivity led Horsup and his colleagues to believe that keeping a northern would be relatively easy. On 22 June 1996, Solstice—a juvenile male known to the scientists as Male 104—was trapped and sent down to Western Plains Zoo to begin a captive breeding program. Similar to the wombat Flinders brought back from Bass Strait, for six weeks Solstice refused to eat and had to be force-fed. Staff would sedate him and then use a syringe to force gruel down his throat. He lost one third of his body weight and in January 1997 he died from a twisted bowel. His death was sudden. He first showed symptoms early in the morning and by that evening he was dead.

'He just used to stand there,' David Blyde told me. 'It was like he was just absolutely bewildered by the whole thing. He just didn't seem to respond to anything. There was no reaction to our presence; no avoidance behaviour.'

Later that year zookeepers caught a second wombat. According to Western Plains Zoo staff, who were alone at the time in Epping Forest, it had entered its trap during the day and its capture was not registered by the radio equipment. By the time it was found the wombat had died from heat exhaustion. It was Male 25—the only northern Horsup had become familiar with. In more than 400 previous captures there had never been such a disaster. The Queensland government, fearful of the consequences of the loss of any more of Australia's rarest mammal, immediately halted plans to establish northern hairy-nosed wombats at Western Plains Zoo, citing the risks as unacceptable. Blyde said that unless the animal was injured or an orphan he would not take on the responsibility of a northern hairy-nosed wombat again. 'Given that we can't breed commons or southerns it's not going to be very useful to try again to breed northerns.'

In spite of nearly a decade of science writing I had never heard these stories nor anything to indicate how dire the northerns' situation is. How was it, I wondered, that the fate of such a beautiful animal on the point of extinction could be so little known?

The environment Horsup and I were walking through was so parched that it reminded me of a vast dried floral arrangement. The dirt was fine and dry, and when disturbed by our vehicles it floated in the air like a red fog. It was clear, however, that the build-up to the wet was coming—huge grey clouds grew thicker and thicker in the skies as the afternoon wore on. The wet season replenishes the landscape, and the entire ecosystem is reliant on its regular arrival. In the early 1990s this region experienced six solid years of drought as one El Niño followed another in unnatural succession. This did nothing to help the northerns. Once the wet arrives the wombats are on their own, since the roads into the park become inaccessible. The trip we were on would be the final survey for 2000.

'This is not how it should look,' Horsup said, waving his arm at all the dried East African grass that was taking over the park. 'I see the buffel grass as a triffid—an invader.'

The buffel grass transforms the landscape and the skyline from the wombat's perspective. It smothers the vegetation that the wombats favour and, even though the northerns eat buffel grass, it is not their preferred food. They eat at least twelve species of grasses or sedge but the biggest proportion of their diet is made up of four native species: three awned grasses, bottle-washer grasses and a local sedge called *Fimbristylis dichotoma*. Out of necessity, however, the weed has become a staple of the marsupials—in 1993 it made up 2 per cent of their diet, and by 1996 more than a quarter. Horsup also fears that the buffel is so thick that it may act like a maze to the wombats when hunted by ferals.

By mid-morning we had made our way to Burrow 30. After a long stretch of silence during which Horsup made notes on his clipboard he became unusually animated. 'Have you ever seen a man get excited about a pile of shit before?'

Just outside the entrance of one tunnel was a northern hairy-nosed wombat turd. It was cubic in shape and the size of the top joint of a man's thumb. It looked as though it had been left there as recently as the previous evening. Fresh poo means living wombats and after the experiences of the last few months a new black cube—the shape baffles scientists—was a welcome sight. Horsup did not hesitate to pick the scat up and break it open as if it were an after-dinner chocolate. When I was at primary school a friend of mine, David

Azzopardi, would take me into his dad's shed to show me a cheese that his family was making. It was hanging from the ceiling and was dripping a clear liquid with such a strong smell it made my eyes water. (I was banned from the Azzopardi home after one of David's friends shot me in the funny bone with an air rifle, but that's another story.) Northern hairy-nosed wombat poo smelt exactly like the Azzopardi family cheese. The dropping Horsup was investigating was bone-dry and as light as pumice stone.

'It's so light because these guys are not drinking,' Horsup told me. 'They're getting all the water out of what they eat. Their metabolic rates are almost reptilian. They may be slow and unspectacular but they have got it worked out.' Wombats have among the lowest water needs of any mammal on Earth—around one-fifth of a sheep's and a quarter of a kangaroo's.

My first book was about the discovery of a new genus of tree called the Wollemi pine—a plant with a fossil history stretching back to the dinosaurs. *Wollemia nobilis* grew all over the Australian continent, but at the time of its discovery at the end of 1994 in a canyon in a wilderness neighbouring Sydney only forty of the trees were remaining. This prehistoric plant tells a bizarre genetic story—each of the trees has identical DNA. Like the wombats, Wollemi pines were first known from fossils and are found alive in a single national park. Unless Wollemi pines are successfully cultivated a single disaster could wipe them out. During my stay at Epping Forest I realised that these trees and northern hairy-nosed wombats share many of the same problems.

'Like the Wollemis the whole hairy-nosed story is here in this one spot,' Horsup said to me when I raised the similarities between these two critically endangered organisms. 'Normally wild animal populations go up and down because of droughts, fires, good times and bad times. But if you have one of these events in a population of a hundred animals you could lose half your breeding females and there may be no recovery from there. It's a bit like a plane that keeps stalling— you lose altitude all the time and you can't get out of the dive. And we know that the next drought is just around the corner.'

The biggest difference between the two organisms is that *Wollemia nobilis* is a botanical superstar, with huge public interest and large amounts of government and private research dollars being spent on its survival. When northern hairy-nosed wombats were attacked and killed in the winter of 2000 they were lucky to get a few column inches in the newspapers.

The deaths of the two wombats during the trapping program and the seven savaged carcasses found in the winter of 2000 effectively mean that any plans of spreading the risk of extinction by establishing another colony elsewhere is even more in doubt. Horsup took me to the spot on the edge of the park where he dumps the decomposing bodies of the wombats killed by dingoes. All he keeps are their skulls. The toughest parts of the animals were still intact even though weeks had passed since their deaths. Their feet and claws looked hard enough to be used as rock-engraving tools. I could still make out a couple of hairy noses in among the mangled mess of the seven bodies. 'This is a very sad sight,' Horsup said. He explained how desperately a dogger—dog hunter—was needed regularly in the park. Horsup's dogger is only able to work in the park for a couple of days every month. Surely, I couldn't stop thinking, an army of doggers should be deployed to Epping Forest, *whatever* the cost. The only possible good news to salvage from such a dreadful situation is that all but one of the dead northerns were male.

In 1993 I wrote a story about the second-last mainland population of little penguins in New South Wales. The birds lived on the far south coast at Eden and on a November evening that year a pack of dogs ate the entire colony. The story was kept secret out of embarrassment until one of my contacts passed the news on to me, appalled that our society should be so reckless with its wildlife. Luckily penguins have safe island populations. The northerns do not have that luxury.

It is a catch-22 situation—the hairy-nosed wombats cannot be secure in the long term if they live in one small section of a tiny national park. But the risks are just too great to move the twelve to eighteen animals required to establish another population—either in captivity or in one of the areas where they were once found. When they are gone it will be a statistic on the conscience of every Australian—as great a loss as the Tasmanian tiger. This loss, however, will not be something we can blame on the ignorance of our forebears. The extinction will occur in our lifetimes or our children's.

'I find it too scary to think about,' Horsup said to me as we sat on the verandah back at camp, waiting for the heat of the middle of the day to moderate. 'When you are working here you tend to forget how desperate this situation is. We don't always make the right decision but we make the best decision possible given all the information available.'

Chapter 9

BURROW CAM

In the winter when the ground was heavy with water, underground work was too dangerous. I occasionally crawled down burrows and usually found the wombat deep down, fast asleep in his nest. This had to be done carefully and no excavating was done. Twice I had very minor cave-ins on my back. During the winter I found four burrows blocked by dirt, and from only one of these burrows did the wombat dig free.

PETER NICHOLSON

In the winter of 1998 after months of planning, the construction of prototypes, and the refining of the best wheel design to travel through the dust and contours of a wombat hole, Alan Horsup's 'burrow cam' was ready. This improvised eye would go where no person had gone before—into the unexplored innards of a yaminon burrow. Camera experts had been consulted, a university engineering department had offered months of technical support and Horsup's curious supervisors were converted to the cause. Nearly sixty years had elapsed since the hairy-nosed wombats at Epping Forest had been discovered and still nobody knew *anything* about their lives underground.

'I dream of an upside-down periscope that allows me to look inside a burrow,' Horsup said. 'I especially dream of seeing a mother with her young. What the hell is a burrow like? Are burrows connected? How long are they? If we are going to establish a captive population successfully we need to know if there are any common characteristics that the animals may need.'

On 20 September 1998 the $3000 burrow cam— $10,000 if the labour hadn't been free—was ready to roll into a landscape more mysterious to scientists than the surface of some of the planets in our solar system. The whole vehicle—machine, camera, radio transmitter, headlights— weighed around five kilograms and was coated with aluminium and stainless steel. A cable attached to the remote-controlled device allowed it to transmit live footage to a television monitor placed at the burrow entrance where Horsup and his colleagues had set up a dusty mission control under a tarp. It was an active burrow and their hope was to spot a wombat. All went well until, at around five metres underground, the explorer snagged and could not be removed. Its radio transmitter, however, allowed the scientists to map the exact spot where it was stuck. An auger was hauled to the site from camp and an afternoon was spent digging. When it broke through into the burrow, however, it pile-drove the top of the vehicle and smashed the radio transmitter. The equipment was retrieved but Horsup was forced temporarily to halt the burrow cam's explorations.

A few months later Horsup's boss in the Queensland parks service, Doug Crossman, was at Epping Forest and they decided to send the device down into Burrow 185—a tunnel that the pair thought would be short and safe. It had the added advantage of being only a couple of metres off the road and under a big tree. Horsup had a bad feeling about the whole exercise but both men agreed that if they limited the burrow cam to no more than five metres into the tunnel then all would probably be OK. At that depth, even without its radio transmitter, the two men were confident they would be able to retrieve the machine. Once again the live television link-up was put in place at the burrow entrance and Horsup and Crossman sent their explorer underground. What they saw as the camera traversed the burrow astonished them. Once the images appeared on their television screen they simply could not stop exploring further.

'It was like a drug,' Horsup recalled as he and I stood at the entrance to Burrow 185 two years after he and Crossman had deployed the burrow cam. 'You have got to see what is around the next corner and then the next.' Contrary to their predictions, the burrow was extraordinarily intricate, with myriad forks, dips, rises, twists, turns and dead ends. 'We could see cave crickets and spiders covering the wall of the burrow and a striped skink which I could identify from the live footage as a sandswimmer.'

Suddenly the transmission ceased. Their elation turned to dismay and then to a desolating sense of loss. Soon afterwards it was apparent that the vehicle had lost power and that the mission was sunk. The blank monitor was as frustrating to them as the radio silence that greeted NASA on a number of its missions to Mars. While NASA is always going to get more funding for its planetary lander vehicles, Horsup knew he would be hard-pressed to get the few thousand dollars for another burrow cam. In their burrow-cam-induced euphoria the scientists had lost track of how much television cable had travelled into the tunnel with the burrow cam. 'We were only

The Secret Life of Wombats

going to go down five metres but when we checked the cable it had gone down seventeen.' They tried, unsuccessfully, to pull it back out and, at that point, the burrow cam might as well have been on the other side of the Moon.

Soon after, part of the cable was shoved to the surface, apparently by a wombat doing a spring-clean. Because of the aridity at Epping Forest, Horsup thought rust was unlikely to be a problem for the burrow cam, and the worst fate he could imagine befalling the vehicle was that a confused wombat might try to push it aside or bury it—a possibility which the engineers had prepared for by making the remote-control vehicle sand- and dust-proof.

Over the next two years, every time Horsup passed Burrow 185, he hoped that one of the wombats would have pushed his burrow cam back to the surface. Two serious rescue missions were attempted and in 1999 precious but futile days were spent digging four-metre holes into the tunnels below. Finally, on one of his drives from Rockhampton to the national park, Horsup stopped at a bargain store called 'Silly Solly's' and purchased a $12.95 plastic front-end loader. This, he decided, would be his reconnaissance vehicle. Back at camp in the national park, he removed the digger and the cabin from the toy truck. A video camera was lashed onto the roof.

Now the only problem was power. Unlike the original

burrow cam, which was fuelled by rechargeable batteries, Silly Solly's tunneller had to be pushed seventeen metres down the burrow using flexible fibreglass poles, which are normally used by telecommunication companies to explore long pipes. The rescue vehicle's mission was to locate the burrow cam so the scientists knew where it was—the issue of retrieval would be dealt with later. Remarkably, the mission was an enormous success—the video camera recorded where the tunnels were heading and gave an approximate location of the burrow cam.

Alan Horsup with the rescue cam which proved that sometimes the cheapest technology works best.

But once again when Horsup and his colleagues dug they found nothing.

One of Horsup's goals during my visit was finally to recover the burrow cam. On the afternoon of Saturday 21 October 2000, assisted by the Green Corps team, he set to work. He promised the workers a reward if they were successful. 'We've got to get it out,' Horsup told them, 'a case of beer is at stake.'

At 3 p.m. digging began. Three hours later the hole was three metres deep but there was no sign of a burrow as we continued to take turns shovelling. Soon, the hole was so deep that the digger was ladling soil into a bucket which was then hauled up to the surface. By nightfall the hole was four metres deep. We had not found the burrow. It was, however, a job the Green Corps preferred to pulling out buffel grass. 'Saving the wombat camera is more interesting than saving the wombat,' was one muffled comment that rose up from deep in the hole.

Hole-digging had worked up a huge thirst. But the Green Corps team was not allowed to bring their own beer out to the forest. Because it is no fun drinking a beer by yourself, in front of people you have been working with all afternoon, I offered my supply. Green Corps co-ordinator Jeff Arneth looked at me as though I had just handed him a ticket around the world. Dennis Steger emptied his stubby in a few gulps: 'Jesus Christ,' he said. 'That would put a horn on a jellyfish.' A couple of hours earlier Horsup had lit a roaring fire, allowing it to burn down to white-hot coals on which he cooked two enormous beef roasts. He and I rigged up an infra-red filter for a spotlight and tested the video camera's night-vision facility. Our plan was to head out spotlighting after dinner.

Around 10 p.m. Jeff, Alan and I set off down hairy-nosed highway. Once again I sat on the bonnet, feet wedged up against the vehicle's bullbar, my butt protected by a shabby bit of foam. The evening was windy and threatening and the air was filled with dust. 'The one thing we know for sure,' Horsup told me, 'is that wombats don't like wind. It confuses them. I don't know whether they become nervous because wind makes it harder to hear predators but we don't usually see native animals on windy nights.' My spotlight lit up the swirling specks of dust as if they were stars.

'Concentrate on the left up here,' Horsup said as we reached the outer limit of the glow of our camp. Even in the dark he knows the location of each burrow. The light swept through the scrub up and down, left to right, right to left, down and up. It is best to hold the spot close in front of your face so light reflecting from an animal's eyes bounces back into your field of vision. As I completed my second or third series of sweeps my spotlight flicked back. What is that? I thought. I swung the light around. I could see a log lying in the knee-high grass. Then I saw the curves of a fat, fur-covered bottom and caught a glimpse of a tiny movement. I knocked on the windscreen behind me and Horsup stopped. A cloud of dust enveloped me as Horsup reversed the vehicle. When the dirt settled the wombat was still there and I felt intense joy at seeing it. I remembered Horsup's advice not to shine the light right on the animal. The beam from the spotlight was tattooing a figure-8 pattern on the landscape just below the wombat. The animal turned around with a startled, embarrassed look on its face, reminding me of a chubby child caught by bullies when a toilet door is flung open. My joy was suddenly tempered by a feeling of guilt that I had disturbed the grazing creature. The animal in my beam was clearly unsure of what to do and I remembered Alan's words earlier in the day when I had asked him whether wombats are smart.

'They're as intelligent as they need to be,' Horsup replied. 'They live down a hole, they come out occasionally to feed—I think they have got all the faculties they need.'

At first the yaminon stood side-on to my beam, motionless. I could see its little legs, the health of its fur. I could see its whisker-covered elongated muzzle and near-blind eyes trying to see through the spotlight. It started to move off away from the beam. Perhaps twenty seconds had passed since my brain had converted a log into a marsupial. I could make out the trail it was following as my beam followed its feet. Its legs reminded me of those of a low coffee table. It was clear, even as it sought to escape the beam, that it was utterly baffled by our sudden arrival. By now it had begun to trot away and I made a noise that, as Horsup put it, got its fast-twitch muscles going. It was as if a rolling boulder had been transformed into a cannonball. In what seemed a fraction of an instant the wombat was gone.

'When they go down in the burrows,' Horsup said, 'they go "woomp, woomp, woomp" and disappear in a cloud of dust. It's no wonder they have hairy noses.'

Everyone had told me how timid these animals are and now I got a real sense of a creature utterly unequipped to deal with humanity. We drove on, sobered by our intrusion, but also excited at seeing such a rare life form. A few minutes later an enormous black-headed python appeared in the middle of the road. It perceived danger and with an impressive flick high-tailed itself off into the bush as if it were a writhing garden hose. (I found out later that black-headed pythons are the only snakes able to dig burrows—turning their heads into a J-shape to shovel.) Less than half an hour later we returned to camp. The lights were out, the fire was a glowing ring of coals, bodies were sprawled asleep all around and we prepared to follow suit. I felt as though Horsup had given me a gift but also a responsibility. 'You are one of the very few people on

Earth to have seen all three species of wombat,' he told me.

'Thank you. Sleep tight,' I replied. In my tent, even with my eyes closed, I could see the hairy-nosed wombat illuminated and motionless.

The next morning, soon after dawn, Horsup and I headed out to continue the burrow surveys. Charcoal clouds filled the sky and showers swept across the desert. We stopped at the spot along the hairy-nosed highway where we had seen the wombat the night before. Horsup estimated that it probably weighed around eighteen kilograms and hence was a juvenile. It did not have an ear tag, which meant it had not been trapped before. It is just such an animal upon which the hopes of the colony now rest.

'People say, "Who cares whether the wombats die? What do they do for us?" Horsup said as we walked from burrow to burrow. 'We have a responsibility to do our utmost to maintain as much diversity as we can. This animal is not going to be out of trouble even in fifty years' time. We are here for the long haul on this one.'

I hope his optimism will be rewarded. As I left Horsup and the Green Corps team that Sunday morning, I also hoped that Epping Forest's burrows would always echo with the sound of 'woomp, woomp, woomp'.

There was one more piece of the puzzle to locate. Nobody would give me a straight answer about what had happened to the northern hairy-nosed wombats of Deniliquin, where the species was recorded until the beginning of last century. Populations were also known from as far afield as Finley, Jerilderie and Tocumwal. The DNA in pelts from these populations matches that of the animals that Alan Horsup is responsible for. But the farmland around Deniliquin is littered with hundreds of former warrens that are today thought to be empty. A small population may have survived until as recently as a decade ago.

The modern history of Deniliquin's wombats begins on 20 December 1861 when an article appeared in the *Deniliquin Pastoral Times*: 'We are informed that Mr James Tyson has succeeded in capturing, or rather killing a wombat; which species of native animal it is said abounds on his station, about 25 miles from Deniliquin. Although a young beast, his dimensions are by no means insignificant, the hide measuring about four feet. The flesh of the wombat is very palatable, and when properly dressed resembles young pork. We have not heard whether the specimen in question has been subjected to culinary processes but we presume that curiosity, at least, would have tempted a gastronomic experiment in his favour.'

Within a decade, Louis Peers, a mysterious wombat hunter and naturalist, had sent skins of these animals to the

This wombat was included in Peter Nicholson's scientific paper. At Timbertop, he would coax the wild wombat he befriended out of its burrow, and visit it underground.

Nicholson dreamed of adventures and revelled in life at Timbertop, where much of the year was spent outdoors, in what remains one of the most rugged wilderness areas on the continent.

Each weekend Timbertop's boys headed off into the wilderness for lengthy, unsupervised hikes. The boys, Peter Nicholson (inset) among them, were all expected to reach the summits of the mountains towering above the school.

'Wherever I am there's always animals,' Nicholson says. 'People tease me because I talk to animals.'

When Peter Nicholson returned to Timbertop in 2001 he found a burrow he had explored and mapped forty years before. He instantly tried to caterpillar inside. 'I'll just go and see whether the turn-around is still there.'

Museum of Victoria. We don't know what happened to that collection but we know from later correspondence with the museum that Peers thought that the Deniliquin wombats were of a different species from the Queensland animals and had the scientific name *Lasiorhinus M'Coy*. On 17 September 1871, Peers wrote to the director of the museum, Sir Frederick M'Coy: 'I have found further species of wombat—(some miles from others) which is rather smaller in size and jet black—the ears I think larger than usual and a very lively animal to what the others are. I have been at this camp twice and have seen five specimens all alike in color—I was not able to procure any not having a gun with me. Do you think this is likely to be a new species. I shall take a trip shortly and try to obtain specimens.'

Peers ended his letter with a question. 'Have you any skins of the Plains Wanderer or skeletons in stock that you would exchange with me for the [wombat] specimen.' In 1883 the museum sent Peers the princely sum of twelve pounds for his Deniliquin specimens. By 1885 he was hunting wombats in Tasmania. History does not tell us whether he ever got his plains wanderer, which is today a desperately endangered bird living in a few small and fragmented populations in the Riverina region of New South Wales.

On 19 January 1884 a grim edict was issued in the *Deniliquin Pastoral Times,* underneath a story about the possible discovery of that mythical Australian beast, the bunyip. 'The Wombat has been declared a noxious animal under the [Pastures and Stock Protection] Act in the Deniliquin District. The Deniliquin Board will, therefore, give a bonus of 5s per each head for the destruction of such animals delivered to the receivers.'

Apart from the bounty, poison baits, catastrophic landscape changes and ignorance caused these populations to collapse rapidly. Throughout the twentieth century it was assumed that the Deniliquin wombats were extinct and that Epping Forest was the species' last stand. In 1981, however, local birdwatcher Philip Maher was in Tuppal State Forest for a spot of exploring when he noticed something strange. The state forest is a near-pristine remnant of the kind of habitat that once covered the district. Big, old trees full of hollows remain as does the understorey. During this visit Maher saw huge amounts of wombat poo, diggings around their burrows and even active wombat trails through the forest.

He sounded the alarm that maybe northern hairy-nosed wombats were not extinct after all. But the wheels of bureaucracy turn slowly and it was not until the mid-1980s that scientists at the Australian Museum, including Tim Flannery and Linda Gibson, travelled to Deniliquin and were guided to the site by Maher. One of Alan Horsup's predecessors at Epping Forest, Doug Crossman, was also on the expedition. It

The Secret Life of Wombats

was very clear that wombats were living in the area, says Flannery. He found scats and saw evidence of digging but spotlighting failed to locate any animals. Two sets of droppings were sent to Barbara Triggs for analysis. When she studied these scats the puzzle deepened. She found possible northern hairy-nosed wombat hair stuck on the outside of the first poo samples. In one of the scats in the second set she found a single common wombat's hair. Some argued that the samples had been contaminated and that the only possible

Tuppal State Forest, June 1985. Heady days for mammalogists as they gathered in Deniliquin to search for wombats. From the left: Tim Flannery, an army volunteer, Philip Maher, Doug Crossman.

explanation was that commons had somehow colonised the district. Flannery wanted to excavate a burrow to solve the riddle but was forbidden.

To this day Dr Linda Gibson, the mammalogist who first alerted me to Peter Nicholson's story, is not prepared to rule out the possibility that the wombats are still somewhere around Deniliquin.

Maher had not been back to the site since 1991 when I asked him if he would take me into the remote forest so that I could see the burrows for myself. I arrived in Deniliquin on a Saturday afternoon in March 2001 and after a short drive out of town we prepared to cross the Edward River. The waterway is a natural barrier. On one side of the river the forest is degraded, littered with rubbish and infested with weeds, but climbing up on the bank on the far side of the river was like entering another world. Tuppal State Forest is a completely different ecosystem from the mountains of Timbertop or anywhere else that commons live. Deniliquin is drier, sandier and flatter—the trees are squat and gnarled compared to the giants further south and to the east. I was immediately reminded of the aridity of Epping Forest.

'This is a place no-one visits much,' Maher said. 'It's one of the most natural areas around Deniliquin. You can tell a real old remnant by the amount of timber on the ground.'

The vegetation may be intact but a whole suite of

mammals that once lived there is now gone. It is another marsupial ghost town. Bilbies, bettongs, quolls, hare wallabies and many others have vanished from Tuppal. The platypuses which once teemed in the river are now rare and the water, once clear and flowing over a sandy riverbed, is so cloudy that you cannot see your hand below the surface. Knee-deep silt sits on the bottom of the river like a dead weight and toxic blue-green algae outbreaks are also a problem.

We began walking under the watchful eyes of noisy, brightly coloured flycatcher birds. Tuppal, fortunately, is still inhabited by a healthy population of forest owls (which probably survive on feral rabbits) and Maher found several tell-tale feathers that had fallen from the predators. Aborigines also once lived in these forests and Maher pointed out a giant four-metre scar on a gum tree, where a hunter had removed bark to construct a canoe. It was the first time I had seen such a relic of Aboriginal river life.

After walking a few hundred metres we came across an old burrow. Debris lay over the entrance and vegetation was growing across the tracks where wombats would once have foraged for food. The enormous spoil mound where the marsupials dumped their dirt after a night's tunnelling was the clearest indicator that the burrow was now lifeless—a crust of moss covered its surface.

'This one was disused even when I found it in 1981,'

After nearly a decade of close study Philip Maher knows all of Tuppal State Forest's burrows.

Maher said. 'I think the trail might have gone cold now.'

The next burrow seemed more recent and Maher spotted a skeleton a metre and a half inside it. My heart started to thump. We climbed into it in turn and yanked at the mummified body. Ribs and skin were still visible, and after a quarter of an hour of pulling we had the body at the surface. The remains were those of some poor kangaroo which had entered the burrow to die or had been chased in there by a predator. It was a very depressing moment. I still held out hope, however, because we had not yet reached the main warren where fifteen years ago the scientists and Maher had found the best indication that hairy-nosed wombats were still in the area.

We passed several other disused burrows and then came across the warren we were looking for. Epping Forest's wombats build their burrows only in sandy soil and that location in Tuppal State Forest had the sandiest soil in the entire area. I might have been standing in Epping Forest itself.

'When this was active you could see runways everywhere,' Maher said. 'You could see the areas where they were grazing and there were diggings all over the place. This is a very sad spot because something could have been done for these animals.'

Maher believes that this population might still be intact if a professional trapper had been allowed to catch a living animal. If this had been done proof of the animal may have ensured adequate funding for their protection. But while the existence of the marsupials remained in doubt, management was impossible and their light was eventually extinguished. Today the forest is slowly reclaiming the wombats' homes and in another few decades it is likely that any sign that these extraordinarily rare creatures once lived by the Edward River will have been erased.

Wombats generally take themselves deep underground to die; under my feet were the bodies of animals that had run out of time in a world where they no longer had a place. They are skeletons in Australia's closet. It was getting late and it was time to head home. I had a forest to walk through, a river to cross and 800 kilometres of highway to traverse before I would step through my front door.

Six weeks later I was reminded of the perilous fate of the northern hairy-nosed all over again. Alan Horsup called me with good and bad news. On 28 April 2001, the burrow cam had been retrieved from its grave in Epping Forest. A second group of Green Corps workers had spent three days excavating. After more than two and a half years underground it had been destroyed by both water, from the holes sunk by Horsup's team, and by wombats, which had chewed big chunks out of the tyres. But Horsup's mood was sombre: he had found another northern had been eaten by a dog.

British palaeontologist Richard Fortey describes in his book *Trilobite* how the ancient arthropods disappeared with a 'whimper'. This makes me think of the fate that will befall the northern hairy-nosed wombat unless we ensure they have a secure home to live their secret lives. 'I am reminded of the piece that Joseph Haydn wrote as a subtle protest against the mean musician's wages at the court of Esterhazy,' Fortey recalled. 'In the final movement of the *Farewell Symphony* the musicians leave one by one, while the music continues vigorously to unfold. In the end a solitary fiddler carries on alone—and only then is there silence.'

Chapter 10

STUCK

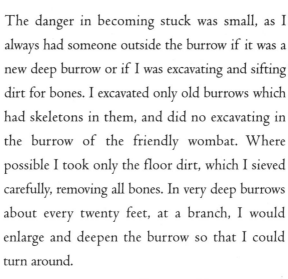

The danger in becoming stuck was small, as I always had someone outside the burrow if it was a new deep burrow or if I was excavating and sifting dirt for bones. I excavated only old burrows which had skeletons in them, and did no excavating in the burrow of the friendly wombat. Where possible I took only the floor dirt, which I sieved carefully, removing all bones. In very deep burrows about every twenty feet, at a branch, I would enlarge and deepen the burrow so that I could turn around.

PETER NICHOLSON

Rod Wells is a passionate soul. He enjoys the thrill of putting his body under the earth into the caverns and crevices that terrify the rest of us. All of his adult life he has been a speleologist—small spaces and becoming stuck hold no fear for him—and a passionate student of wombats. He is small, bearded and, today, mostly grey, rather like a neat, thin Santa Claus. Some people are not what they appear but Wells looks like a wombat scientist. He is the world's foremost expert on the southern hairy-nosed species and, after Nicholson, was the first person to undertake behavioural studies of the animals. Prior to the schoolboy's study at Timbertop and Wells' work, research on wombats had focused almost totally on taxonomy.

Wells planned to study bandicoots until Professor Peter Crowcroft—the man whose name is attached to the most ancient of the fossil wombat-like creatures that are found at Riversleigh and in South Australia, *Rhizophascolonus crowcroftii*—took him on a road trip to see southern hairy-nosed wombats in the wild. Wells was absorbed by the creatures, fascinated by the fact that such a large mammal was surviving in conditions of extreme aridity. South Australia is the driest state on the continent, with vast areas subject to extreme conditions. His early studies explored how wombats survive in the desert where ground temperatures exceed 50 degrees Celsius.

Even today, many of the simplest biological facts about

southerns are unknown. The creature was first described from a skull in 1849. The hairy-nosed genus was not formally established, however, until 1863, based on a South Australian wombat living at London Zoo.

In December 1971 Wells, a thirty-one-year-old doctoral student, was conducting field work on a private property near Blanchetown, crawling down burrows that reminded him of scaled-down calderas. He was deploying thermohydrographic monitors in these tunnels to measure temperature and humidity.

Wells was staying with a sheep farmer named Ray Dorward and because he was working on his own had notified the grazier of the area he would be investigating that day. About midday he wriggled down inside the cone at the entrance to a tunnel. Southerns are the smallest of the wombat species—typically weighing only twenty-five kilograms—and the entrance that Wells had to push himself into was impossible to enter with his shoulders square and both arms held in front. Instead, one arm, holding the thermohydrograph, was held forwards and the other was pressed down by his side. Even in such an awkward position and in spite of Wells' small frame he was wedged against the walls of the tunnel. To make matters worse this was a steep burrow. Wells also knew that southerns often share their tunnels with one of the most deadly and aggressive Australian

Rod Wells and friend. Wells is the world's foremost expert on southern hairy-nosed wombats.

snakes—the king brown. Soon his entire body was inside the burrow. From the surface the only sign of his presence was his parked four-wheel-drive a hundred metres away. He was pushing the thermohydrograph ahead of himself and had reached a depth of a couple of metres underground and a few metres inside when he decided he had gone far enough. With his free hand he began to dig a niche in the burrow wall to put the device into where it would not be disturbed by a wombat. A few seconds later his problems began. He started to wriggle

The Secret Life of Wombats

backwards but each time he struggled rubble fell down the steep tunnel. Soon he was wedged in, and could go neither forwards nor backwards. Every time he moved, the scree packed him in tighter. In front of his face it was pitch-black. There was nothing he could do except wait until someone came to look for him. An hour passed, then a second, a third and a fourth. He could hear noises inside the burrow and knew that if a wombat decided to attack he would be completely vulnerable. If a king brown tried to slither past he would certainly be killed. In such circumstances scorpions, spiders or any of a dozen other desert hazards didn't even rate a thought.

In July 1997 I covered the rescue of Stuart Diver from rubble after the catastrophic Thredbo landslide. Diver lay beside the body of his dead wife for sixty-three hours beneath hundreds of tonnes of mud and concrete. As the rescuers dug I watched one corpse after another being pulled from the wreckage. I also saw the look of joy on Diver's face when he was brought to the surface and took his first breath of fresh air. I remember his stunned expression at seeing stars in the sky before he was loaded onto a helicopter and flown to Canberra.

That moment gave me a tiny insight into how rescue from burial must feel. For many people being buried alive is the most frightening way to die imaginable. In his tale 'The Premature Burial' Edgar Allan Poe captures the feeling: 'The unendurable oppression of the lungs—the stifling fumes of the damp earth—the clinging of the death garments—the rigid embrace of the narrow house—the blackness of the absolute Night—the silence like a sea that overwhelms—the unseen but palpable presence of Conqueror Worm—these things, with the thought of the air and the grass above, with memory of dear friends who would fly to save us if informed of our fate, and with consciousness that of this fate they can *never* be informed—that our hopeless portion is that of the really dead—these considerations, I say, carry into the heart which still palpitates, a degree of appalling and intolerable horror from which the most daring imagination must recoil. We know nothing so agonising upon Earth—we can dream of nothing half so hideous in the realms of the nethermost Hell.'

Perhaps it was fortunate that Wells had not read Poe. He kept his head and remained patient. He tried to recall the precise instructions he had given the farmer about where he would be working. Several hours after Wells was due back, Dorward became worried about the enthusiastic young scientist on his property and did go looking. He quickly found the four-wheel-drive but could see no sign of its driver. To a sheep farmer the idea that anyone would voluntarily go down a wombat burrow was total lunacy. He did, however, have an inkling of what this crazy marsupial expert was capable of and started calling his name.

One of the problems that confronted Dorward is that a southern hairy-nosed wombat colony has dozens of entrance tunnels spread out over hundreds of square metres. Wells could be down any one of these holes. Eventually, however, the farmer heard a muffled reply to his calls and on looking further could see Wells' feet wriggling inside the darkness of the tunnel. Dorward clambered down into the caldera and started to pull but discovered how tightly Wells had got himself stuck. He walked back to his truck and returned to the hole armed with a rope. Once again he climbed down but this time he slung a knot over Wells' ankles and pulled with all his might. Twenty minutes later, grazed, blinded by the light after four hours of darkness and sheepish about his narrow escape, Wells was back above ground. He had learnt one important scientific fact from his imprisonment—even in the middle of the day, in the middle of a desert, a wombat burrow does not get hot. Of all the emotional and physical discomforts he experienced that day, heat exhaustion was not among them—no wonder wombats were able to thrive in such an arid environment. In spite of his scare, Wells was not daunted and went on to publish dozens of scientific papers on wombats.

Rod Wells dominated Australian southern hairy-nosed wombat research until 1994, when he organised the first ever

Almost his entire life Ron Dibben's major source of protein has been wombat.

conference on wombats. For Wells the meeting was a symbolic end to his quarter-century of researching southerns. He passed the baton to Melbourne Zoo's Peter Temple-Smith, who in turn employs one of the most colourful characters ever associated with the creatures. Ron Dibben, an old wombat shooter, is a key figure in the scientific effort to understand the southern hairy-nosed species. All who work with him speak with awe of his passion for wombats and his deep knowledge of how they live in the arid areas of South

The Secret Life of Wombats

Australia. Dibben is a large man, fifty-eight years old, and with his wife Ingrid operates research camps for Temple-Smith, who is trying to breed hairy-nosed wombats in captivity. The work involves some highly complicated and controversial procedures including a technique called cross-fostering. This involves taking a pouch young from its mother's teat and attaching it to the teat of another female. The aim is that one day young can be removed from a northern hairy-nosed teat and attached to a southern mother. This would allow the northern to produce another young in the same year, doubling its breeding success.

Not everyone is convinced that cross-fostering northerns will work, or is even appropriate, but the captive breeding effort has become more and more important as the northerns teeter towards extinction. At the end of March 2001 the Queensland government announced that a special breeding facility would be constructed in Rockhampton, which would initially house southerns but one day, hopefully, northerns too. Wombats are one of the world's most difficult animals to captive breed. After nearly a decade of effort Melbourne Zoo has bred only two. When a captive bred animal is born it is, Temple-Smith admits, still something of a fluke.

'No-one in the world has been able to say successfully "we are going to breed a wombat this year" and then do it,' Temple-Smith told me. A few years ago Melbourne Zoo thought it had cracked the puzzle of breeding hairy-nosed wombats when it was discovered that the females' ovulation is closely related to the appearance of new feed after rain. Grass germination was stimulated for the captive females and a wombat was born. The next year the same approach was taken and there were no young. Only Wells has had any consistent success. Years ago he placed a southern hairy-nosed pen outside his kitchen window so he could observe the animals while he cooked or did the dishes. He successfully bred seven joeys.

Dibben has been a member of the Melbourne Zoo's research team for eight years. According to him a single colony can turn a hectare of land into a moonscape of pits, burrows and denuded vegetation. In his life he estimates that he has shot in excess of 10,000 southern hairy-nosed wombats. There were periods when he shot a hundred wombats a night for weeks on end and the only meat he ate was wombat: wombat roast, wombat stew, wombat soup, wombat mince, wombat drumsticks and wombat sandwiches. The best recipe he knows is to place a prime cut of wombat into a camp oven with a teacup full of water, oil, dripping, Worcestershire sauce, salt and pepper. The pot is then covered in ashes and left to bake. The hindquarter cut is the best and the prime size for tenderness is when a wombat is still a juvenile weighing between twelve and fifteen kilograms.

The Secret Life of Wombats

Lasiorhinus latifrons is the southern hairy-nosed wombat. It has silky fur, a pig-like snout, long pointed ears and is one of the most arid-adapted mammals on Earth.

Dibben has eaten wombats with Aborigines, who throw their wombats whole onto the fire, singe off the hair and then eat the flesh extremely rare. 'I have eaten wombat all my life and people always say it tastes like this or it tastes like that— but it tastes like wombat,' Dibben told me. 'I like to gnaw it off the bone and then charcoal the bones over the fire because I like my charcoal.'

He still has a licence to shoot 150 southerns a year but his great love is helping scientists mount their expeditions into wombat strongholds. His involvement with the scientists has helped him to see the animals in a different light. 'I am much more conservation-minded now,' Dibben said, 'because they're a unique animal in Australia. Even though we have got hundreds of thousands they're just in this one civilisation here in Australia and nowhere else in the world.'

Like an outback William Tell, Dibben's job and that of his team is to fire a bullet from a .22 rifle between a wombat's ears, centimetres above its head. Dibben and colleagues usually dispatch bullets from the back of his 1972 HQ Holden ute, which is mounted with lights and rifles as well as bars and traps. No-one knows why, but when a bullet grazes a wombat's head it will almost always sit still, enabling researchers to creep up behind the marsupial and sling their nets over it. Temple-Smith's team has asked army ballistic experts why the William Tell stunning method works. Perhaps, they say, the wombats are rendered senseless by a compression wave. Dibben believes the bullets leave the animals deaf long enough for them to be captured and examined. Hundreds of wombats are stunned in this way, and only once or twice a year does Dibben kill one by mistake.

One of the highlights of Dibben's career, he told me, was watching the moment of creation of life. The scientists had brought a 'big powerful' microscope out into the desert. A female was captured and her reproductive tract flushed. The fluid was placed under the microscope. Dibben watched the male sperm entering the female egg. He has seen joeys the size of a baked bean and once he even saw twins in a female's pouch.

Dibben's experience with wombats is vast. Once he was hurtling through the scrub in pursuit of a big specimen that suddenly careered off to the side of the Holden, colliding head-on with a mallee stump. There was a sickening thud and the wombat rose up on its hind legs, fell backwards and died, like something out of a Road Runner cartoon. Every hubcap on his ute has been damaged in collisions with southerns. On another occasion he swears that he saw a wombat leap over a metre-high fence. He says that people who regard them as cute and cuddly are wrong. 'They're savage,' he insists. A wombat once bit a chunk out of his leg the diameter of a fifty-cent piece. For Dibben the ultimate skill for any animal is to survive, and that is the mark of a wombat's intelligence. 'They're very intelligent because they exist where nothing else can. They have the ability to live and breed on nothing.' The metabolism of southerns is so slow that some scientists joke they might as well be dead considering the pace at which they digest their dinners. 'In the middle of a drought there's not a blade of grass anywhere out here—not even dead blades of grass and yet the wombats are fat and healthy,' Dibben told me. 'When we dissect their stomachs they are full of green grass no matter how dry it is.'

Wells solved the food puzzle that Dibben and others had encountered by getting down on his hands and knees during a drought in a South Australian desert, when the landscape 'looked like the surface of Mars'. He discovered that even in the driest of times, tiny green shoots could be found deep within dead tufts of native grass and found that in these hot, dry periods southerns could retreat into their burrows and drop their body temperatures, which put their metabolisms into a lower gear. Wells also made another, more staggering discovery—home ranges of southerns are fewer than four hectares. A macropod of the same size as a wombat needs 380 hectares. Common wombats need fourteen hectares, and northerns, with core areas of four to six hectares, have a maximum range of twenty-five. And, as regards feeding times, northerns spend no more than six hours a night grazing and sometimes only two. By comparison, an eastern grey kangaroo must feed for between ten and eighteen hours each day to survive.

In 1994, Peter Temple-Smith and colleagues Vernon Steele and Dave Taggart had the opportunity to open up the burrows of a colony of southern hairy-nosed wombats near Fowlers Bay in South Australia, when a farmer decided to turn a 200-hectare paddock into crop land. The scientists were invited to catch the marsupials so they could be relocated and their tunnel systems excavated and studied. The longest burrow was more than sixty metres—more than twice the maximum recorded in any burrow dug by common wombats, and the deepest was four metres underground. The shapes of the tunnels of the three species of wombats are also very different, probably reflecting different soil types. Southerns and northerns tend to have ellipsis-shaped burrow entrances whereas commons are often an upside down U-shape.

Glenn Shimmin and Russell Baudinette from the University of Adelaide have found that an enormous amount of energy is expended in digging forty-two kilograms of dirt in fifty minutes—the equivalent to fifteen centimetres of tunnel. The pair calculated that the oxygen used to excavate this dirt was 12,000 times greater than walking the same distance. At that rate a ten-metre tunnel would take around eighty hours of vigorous digging and expend more energy than walking 120 kilometres. The largest warrens the scientists have investigated have over a hundred metres of tunnelling and are probably many centuries old.

Not everybody finds southern wombats interesting or thinks these creatures should be the faunal emblem of South Australia. Allen Stott, who runs a cereal farm in the far west of South Australia, fifteen kilometres west of Ceduna, describes them as 'a worse pest than European rabbits because their massive warrens are more difficult and expensive to destroy', and agrees with Tim Flannery's argument that commercial utilisation of wombat meat could make control more economical.

Until 1971 wombats had a bounty on their heads in Victoria and were labelled as vermin through to 1984. Sixty thousand bounties were paid between 1929 and 1955. Nearly 50,000 pounds worth of bounties were forked out in the seven years prior to 1966. Just as the vermin label was lifted, however, wombats were declared unprotected wildlife in 193 parishes in the east of the state. According to Ian Temby, the bio-diversity program officer in the Victorian Department of Natural Resources and Environment, the culling of wombats under this declaration even allowed landholders to control wombats one kilometre inside neighbouring crown land. As late as 1969 newspapers ran headlines like: 'HOW MANY WOMBATS PER LB. OF CYANIDE?' above stories reporting the massive use of poisons—478 kilograms of cyanide in the Mitta Mitta district alone. In 1969 the *Sun* newspaper—a metropolitan daily—ran a banner headline: 'PLAGUE OF WOMBATS—AS BIG AS PIGS'.

By 1912 in South Australia wombats were put in the same category as foxes, hares, feral cats, rabbits, wild dogs, rats and mice as members of the unprotected wildlife club. In

1964 full protection, except for damage-control purposes, was conferred on the state's wombats. They were declared noxious in parts of New South Wales right through until 1959—farmers were actually obliged to destroy them. After 1959 the wombats were unprotected in the state but no longer noxious. In 1973 the common wombat was finally given full protection.

In Queensland wombats were protected from as long ago as 1906, but permits for destruction were still obtainable. In the Australian Capital Territory there is no provision for the destruction of wombats. Common wombats were declared vermin in Western Australia at the end of the 1960s in spite of the fact that the species does not survive there. Even the southern hairy-nosed wombats have barely got a toehold in that state. Behind the Western Australian legislation is the fear that wombats could be introduced into the wheat-belt regions of that state. Wombats were unprotected in Tasmania until 1970 and even today landholders are able to obtain yearly permits to shoot up to 400 of the animals on their land. Yet thousands of common wombats are still shot there illegally each year.

Southern hairy-nosed wombats once ranged from south-western Victoria and the Murray River floodplains in New South Wales right through to the western extreme of the Nullarbor Plain. Today the majority live in the Nullarbor and the west coast of South Australia; already geographically isolated, the southerns are becoming increasingly genetically distinct.

These genetic and geographical concerns are further exacerbated by the climate and Wells sounds a note of warning about this. It takes as many as three consecutive good years of rain for a baby wombat to reach adulthood. Further reducing the likelihood of this occurring is the fact that these rains must fall in April to ensure there is green grass at the time of weaning: there have been only twenty years in the past century where the weather in the southerns' range facilitated the joey's chance of survival. As there is no way of estimating the age of a wombat, Wells fears that because of this climate roulette, combined with competition and habitat change, many of South Australia's wombats may be deceptively elderly. And when these animals die the species may crash.

Chapter 11

THE DEVIL'S KITCHEN

If the wombat finds a deserted burrow, which may
contain the dead body of another wombat, it will
dig either another tunnel or widen the burrow to
by-pass the dead wombat. It will not disturb a
fairly fresh dead wombat but will toss the bones
around if only the skeleton is left.

PETER NICHOLSON

It was ten days since my trip to Epping Forest and I was in the far north of Tasmania to spend a few days at Narawntapu National Park. Narawntapu is an antidote to Epping Forest—so many wild wombats fill the park that from a distance the marsupials resemble miniature herds of bison on an American prairie. The park centres on a peninsula that juts out into Bass Strait, with low-lying land on either side, stretching from one headland to another like webbing between the fingers of a frog. Much of this country was swampland before the Europeans' arrival but it was quickly drained and turned over to stock. The cattle and sheep are now gone and the reclaimed land is occupied by great mobs of marsupials. I had travelled to the park because it is the nearest ecosystem to an African plain that Australia has in terms of the variety and quantity of wildlife. It is also the best place on Earth to see wild wombats and the Tasmanian animals that prey on them.

I spent several hours each day on one of the plains where the wombats thrive. What is remarkable is that while the common wombat on the mainland is almost universally a nocturnal animal, Narawntapu's population are out grazing day and night. On some days it is possible to see nearly a hundred feeding in one place at lunchtime. The grass was the most lawn-like wild place I had ever seen, with almost every blade neatly nibbled. During my visit there were always around thirty and all were oblivious to my presence. It was apparent how poor their eyesight is. If I sat absolutely still the marsupials would graze closer and closer until they were almost underfoot before realising that a person was nearby. Then their demeanour would change to bristling silence or angry hissing. Rod Wells had told me that the best way to get close to a wombat is to take advantage of its poor binocular vision. A person approaching from directly in front is almost invisible to a wombat.

By sitting on just one log for a few hours at Narawntapu it is possible to see a kaleidoscope of wombat behaviour that scientists working in other parts of Australia take an entire career to witness. Feeding, fighting, swimming, competing with other marsupials, burrowing, grooming and caring for young are all on display. Babies wandered at the heels of their mothers and two males held a hiss-off that degenerated into a rumble over a prime patch of grass beside a freshwater lake. Another fed on a tiny spit of soggy land that nosed out into the estuary. I was struck not only by the diurnal behaviour of these wombats but also by the enormous variety in their colour—from almost gloss-black to that of sand. Their fur seemed longer than that of mainland wombats as it ruffled in the sea breezes that whistled across the park's plains. The fauna backdrop to the wombats consisted of large numbers of kangaroos and wallabies and often all three grazed together. An echidna, an egg-laying mammal, waddled by and I was surprised to notice how similar its gait was to the nearby wombats. I was reminded of a comment made by Anna Gillespie, a researcher studying ancient fossils collected from Riversleigh. 'The incredible thing about Australian animals,' she had said, 'is if you just change a bone here and there you can make a wombat into a completely different marsupial.'

I also thought about Peter Nicholson's words of forty years ago. The young wombat scientist was struck by two things, as I was in northern Tasmania: how strange it seemed for wombats to be grazing in the middle of the day and how interesting that there were so many variations in their appearance.

'I always thought wombats were completely nocturnal and very much alike, but they show a lot of divergence in their behaviour,' Nicholson recorded. 'I often saw wombats out playing and feeding at all times during the day, provided there was not much sun. In an area of over a hundred square miles I found many different wombat communities.

Just before dusk on my second night on the Tasmanian coast, Nick Mooney, wildlife management officer with Tasmania's nature conservation branch, unceremoniously dropped a dead thirty-kilogram common wombat onto its back beside a stagnant pool of water. He reached for a thumb-width, metre-long piece of steel which he bashed into a U-shape. On a small hill just behind him was a large exotic pine, with a tent hanging from its lower branches. This would be used later in the evening as a place for us to hide. In the lee of the tree was an old homestead—for 140 years Narawntapu had been a farm—now inhabited by the park's ranger.

Mooney, a tall man with wild hair and wilder eyes, reached for a knife and with it sliced the wombat open. Using the back of an axe he hammered the inverted steel U into the cavity left by the removal of the wombat's intestines, straddling the backbone. Hammered down in this way, the wombat was firmly secured to the soaked ground. Mooney then rigged a light on a pole and pointed it directly at the wombat. Now he manhandled out a second stinking wombat body from behind another tree and, using a foul piece of rope, tied it. Mooney was working fast but I had to ask him where he had found the wombats. During the three-hour drive from Hobart to the national park, he explained, he had found four dead wombats, all of them roadkill.

'I am going to drag this one up there and bring it back to create a scent trail,' Mooney said. As he hauled the second wombat across the plain, blood and guts wiped onto the grass. He set off at a fast lope, following the base of the hill, with the wombat dragging along behind him.

'I don't want there to be any distractions,' he said, again apparently to himself, before pointing at his blood-covered knife. 'Pick that up, will you?' I bent over, gingerly holding it between thumb and forefinger, and followed him up the hill.

By 8.30 p.m. the last light from the sun had been replaced by that from Mooney's spotlights, creating a glow around the dead wombat. The wind was so strong that it was deafening and, as on the evening I had spotlit the northern hairy-nosed wombat with Alan Horsup, the gale was making the marsupials fidgety. In the dimness I saw a spectre move towards the wombat and soon it was on top of the carcass, frenzied as if it were murdering the dead animal. Mooney crept up to the pine tree on the hill thirty metres from the staked-out carcass and a quarter of an hour later I followed him.

Twenty metres below us a Tasmanian devil—a female, Mooney said, and probably with denned pups judging by the way she was gorging herself—was on top of the wombat, tearing at its entrails, ripping away fur, cleaving through bone, using its hind legs to attempt to wrest the wombat away from its stake. Five other devils were snarling and hissing around in the periphery of the light. Several of these were male, and much bigger than the feasting female. Each time one of the devils approached, the female lunged, screaming and flashing her fangs. Each time the challenger backed off, tail down, snarling in frustration. Each time the female returned to the wombat and resumed her mauling. In spite of the apparent ferocity of the scene before me much of the racket is theatre—devils prefer their own company and when they are

The Secret Life of Wombats

forced together they use complex behavioural displays to assert themselves. They are also biologically amazing—mothers give birth to their young after a gestation of a mere twenty days—and they are the largest living carnivorous marsupials in the world.

Mooney had set up telescopes in the tent under the tree, and looking through one I could see the devil's eyes glowing in the reflected light as if fired by evil. Her entire face was glistening with blood and it seemed she hissed through her snout to clear her nostrils of offal. Left undisturbed, a devil can consume 40 per cent of its body weight in just half an hour. Courtesy of a radio transmitter near the dead wombat we could hear the slurping, fighting and cracking of bones. Devils have jaws five times more powerful than a dog their size and their muscle-bound cheeks are a striking facial feature.

The female's pace began to flag. Her stomach was so full that she appeared almost as wide as she was long, as if she had swallowed a tyre. She was joined at the wombat's side by another devil, then a third, a fourth, a fifth and finally a sixth. One of these was a pup who looked extremely nervous being near the adults. Tasmanian devils give the impression that they will eat anything. Mooney is often called by Tasmanian police to suicide scenes that have been disturbed by devils. At one, a man had hanged himself from a tree at Cradle Mountain and

Tasmanian devils are black and white for camouflage purposes and, although they don't hunt in packs, the power of their jaws in relation to their size is similar to the African hyena.

the devils had managed to eat his shoes off. They have such sturdy constitutions that Mooney has even found echidna spines in devil scats. On another occasion part of his own boot turned up in devil poo after Mooney had dropped bacon on its toe and left it outside his tent before going to bed.

A disfigured devil—dubbed 'Elvis'—was probably the dominant devil of this group, Mooney told me. Elvis' cheeks and neck were mangled from years of successful devil love-making in which the female lets the male know she has had

The Secret Life of Wombats

enough by attacking her partner. There was no love me tender here. 'They have very strong immune systems,' Mooney said. 'I have seen living male devils with jawbones exposed from where they have been attacked by a female.'

As the animals took up positions on the wombat, Mooney directed my attention to their vast whiskers, which are longer than their faces are wide. He believes this allows them to sense where their neighbours are gnawing and to avoid being inadvertently attacked. For the next three hours the devils stripped and crunched the wombat. The scene before me was unlike anything that I had witnessed anywhere in Australia and was akin to a pride of lions tearing apart a wildebeest.

The devils dropped away in turn until by about 1 a.m. only one animal remained, trying to tear nourishment out of the empty shell of the wombat. Mooney cracked open a beer as we watched the final scenes of the devils' kitchen. 'This is a throwback scene to a time before the arrival of Europeans,' he said. 'It's the volume of animals. None of them is unhealthy. They cannot afford to be. With this density of devils you don't get a chance to stay sick.'

As we watched the last devil mop up the feast Mooney told me his theory that this place was Australia's Serengeti. He had even done some back-of-envelope calculations to prove it. 'On this three square kilometres in front of us,' Mooney said, pointing into the darkness, 'there would be thirty devils. At six kilograms each that's 180 kilograms of carnivores. That's a lion or three or four hyenas.' Adding up the weight of the wallabies and wombats he came up with a thumbnail figure of eleven tonnes of herbivores, invisible in the darkness. One evening nine years ago Mooney, using night glasses, counted a hundred eastern grey kangaroos, 900 wallabies and thirty-seven wombats. Every night those thirty devils need to replace 15 per cent of their body weight with prey. That means every night six to eight 'wallaby equivalents' fall prey to the same kind of feasting Mooney had staged.

Not only devils pose a threat to wombats in Tasmania—in the nest of a pair of sea eagles on Flinders Island Mooney found five wombat skulls. 'These creatures know what great food wombat is,' Mooney told me. 'The convicts that escaped from Tasmanian prisons had a saying: "You can go further on less wombat than anything else."'

Nick Mooney is now training enthusiastic farmers around the state to value the wildlife on their properties rather than kill it. Thousands of devils and wombats are still shot illegally every year in Tasmania, often for no better reason than that is what farmers' fathers and grandfathers before them did. Mooney once found twenty-seven dead devils dotted around a poisoned sheep carcass. Devils do in fact play a vital role in clearing away carrion. Mooney believes that

The Secret Life of Wombats

locals can make money out of marsupials. Part of the reason he puts on the devil kitchens is to prove to people that Tasmanian devils are capable of a performance worth paying to see. To date as many as 400 people have seen these shows.

We finished our beers and walked out onto the plain, travelling in an arc to get downwind of the Tasmanian devil. It was so mesmerised by its food that we were able to get within a few metres before it noticed us and fled. It moved so fast it risked outpacing its shadow. At other times, when there has been less wind, Mooney has been able to sit in a chair beside the feast. On one occasion he lay on his chest and pulled himself right up to the carcass he had staked out, his head next to those of the devils. As long as he stayed low, he said, his presence was tolerated.

'Why is this national park like this? So different from the rest of Australia?' I asked him. 'This seems so strange.'

'This is not abnormal. This is how it should be,' Mooney replied. 'The animals are not shot here or harassed. There's no dogs, dingoes and foxes and because there's no road near the park there's no roadkill.'

Before Aborigines and Europeans arrived much of Tasmania would have been like this, with one important exception. Until a few generations ago thylacines ruled these wilds. Mooney says that devils are not big enough to claim the mantle of top-order predator. But even in the absence of a higher predator at Narawntapu, the devils there hold a residual fear of thylacines so powerful it echoes on these plains more than sixty years after Tasmanian tigers became extinct. At that moment we heard the screech of a quoll—the carnivore on the rung below the devils.

We walked over to what was left of the wombat. Its head had been turned inside out and all that was left of its body was skin and fur. Scattered around were a few shards of bone. It was as if the wombat had swallowed a bomb. I walked back to the shed and took ages to fall asleep. By the morning nothing was left of the wombat whatsoever.

Three nights later I was with one of the farmers who had been trained by Mooney, Geoff King. He is a gentle, passionate, talkative north-west Tasmanian and his family have farmed at Marrawah on the coast for over 120 years. In 1996 he and his brother decided to divide the land they had inherited. King's idea was to manage his half for conservation. He met Mooney by chance in a pub and immediately fell in love with the idea of bringing people to see the wildlife that thrives on his land. Today, only a few years since he and his brother separated their family business, King says the gap between what he earned as a cattle farmer and what he earns from showing people devils is 'not that great'. While staying at his shack I was able to creep right up to a carcass during a devil feast until I was almost cheek by jowl with the predators. For a strange moment I had a sense of what it must feel like to be tearing apart a wombat.

In early 2001 one of Narawntapu's wombats was discovered with mange, a disease previously undetected in the national park's population. If it spreads wombat numbers will plummet and the entire ecosystem there will be impacted.

Chapter 12

MOUNT TIMBERTOP

In an area of over a hundred square miles I found many different wombat communities. Along the Howqua River the wombats were brown-furred and ferocious. In the King River–Mount Buttercup area they were a dark grey and played around a lot during the day. In the Mount Buller–Mount Timbertop area they were a light grey, fairly inactive, friendly type.

PETER NICHOLSON

A crash splintered saplings in the scrub as a flash of fur fled Peter Nicholson's approach. 'There goes a wallaby,' he called. He got closer, saw the squat body and bristly jet-black pelt and whispered with a trace of alarm that it was not a wallaby but rather a feral pig. A few metres closer and the big, bare, leathery nose, the curve of its rear end and tiny cetacean-like eyes gave away its true identity. 'It's a wombat,' Nicholson said in hushed tones.

It was late afternoon on 8 March 2001. The temperature was well over 30 degrees Celsius. More than forty years had passed since Nicholson was a student at Timbertop and he had not visited since. I had never before been to that part of Victoria's high country that towers over bushranger Ned Kelly's old haunts of Merrijig and Mansfield. We had been planning the trip for weeks and I was relieved and excited to be in the place where modern Australian wombat research began. I had picked Nicholson up early that morning from Albury airport in high spirits.

At Timbertop Nicholson was greeted like a returning hero, asked to sign a poster project done by a student about 'the Wombat Man' and shown through the school's museum. After a long chat with the Timbertop archivist, Helen Bohren, we changed clothes, grabbed our torches and headed off for an afternoon of exploring the exact locations where Peter had done his wombat research back in 1960 as a fifteen-year-old.

The Secret Life of Wombats

First we passed D Unit, the dormitory from which Nicholson had escaped on countless evenings to do his research. We crossed the creek below the dorm and within seconds the school was obscured by forest. We walked only a few metres upstream and Peter found the burrow where he had done most of his mapping and excavating. He clambered down the tunnel as far as he could fit and was exploring the darkness with his torch.

'It's smaller than I remembered,' Nicholson said. 'I'll just reach in and see whether the turnaround is still there. It's very clear no children have been down here for years.' Nicholson caterpillared himself inside the burrow. 'This is the action,' he said, his voice muffled from within. He caterpillared back out.

I got down onto my chest and entered the hole. A steady, cool, soft breeze blew from its invisible depths. The curved, carved walls were similar to the interior of an underground hotel I had once stayed in during a visit to the opal-mining town of Coober Pedy in central Australia. Their colour was identical to milky coffee. Tiny roots protruding from the wall of the burrow had been neatly gnawed back so they were flush with the tunnel. Bits of rock were also embedded in the walls and the floor was dry and soft and very dusty. It was from these soil deposits on the floor that Nicholson had sieved his skeleton. A cloud of dust lifted as I exhaled but there was no smell whatsoever, just the dry coolness that I have felt in outback wine cellars. The thought of going in made me claustrophobic. A wombat tunnel is a place that I know I will never explore, even if I were ever skinny enough actually to get inside one. I caterpillared out the way Nicholson had shown me and said, 'How the hell did you get inside there?'

'I weigh fourteen stone now,' Nicholson replied. 'I only weighed nine stone then. It was always a squeeze but as long as you could only feel the burrow wall against one shoulder it was OK. When you could feel pressure on both sides that was when you were in trouble.'

Four decades earlier a group of boys had climbed into that particular turnaround. It was clear that the burrow was now long abandoned. There was no dung near its entrance, no scratchings, no runways leading into the blackness and no tracks in the dust at the front door.

We decided to push on and had just started walking when we startled the wombat. It continued to push through the dense thicket of blackberry that covered the banks of Timbertop Creek. In a few seconds it would have disappeared from view, swallowed up by the understorey of the giant forest all around the creek.

'Hmmpphh, hmmppphh, hmmpphhh,' Nicholson muttered. His head lowered on the 'H' part of the grunt and rose on the 'pphhh'. The noise came from the back of his throat and sounded almost as though he was clearing it.

Bolting for its hole, the wombat had reached the runway leading to the entrance when Nicholson started grunting. It slowed and then stopped, and then cautiously began to turn its head. It backed up, moving away from the safety of the burrow.

Nicholson signalled me forward. I crept past him as he continued making his soft grunts. Prickles cut my arms and hands. By now I was so close to the wombat that if I had wanted to I could have touched its back. I could make out the individual bristles on its vast rump. Its fur was the colour of darkness—the only jet-black wombat that I had ever seen. Its ears were chewed—a good indicator that this big specimen was a male who had been in many fights over females. He stared at me and I felt a very strange sensation. The encounter was almost too weird to be true. This was the place where Nicholson had shown the science master his wombat field research. I had spent time with many of Australia's most respected wombat scientists and none of them was able to bring me as close to a wild wombat. 'It's uncanny, isn't it?' Nicholson whispered.

I pushed my luck by trying to get even closer in order to photograph the marsupial's face but it had decided enough was enough. It ambled down its hole, its pigeon-toed feet disappearing into the darkness. Nicholson was smiling from ear to ear.

We were just metres away from the home of the young wombat which Nicholson had made friends with when he was a boy. It was possible that the old male we had just encountered was related to that animal. Perhaps their lives had overlapped. 'They would almost certainly be from the same gene pool,' Nicholson told me.

Later we were told by school staff that a number of students had reportedly spotted a wild pig disappearing into the scrub. No-one, however, had been able to get close enough to the suspected 'pig' to confirm its identity. No doubt it was the same old fellow we had been sitting with.

We continued hiking up towards the headwaters of Timbertop Creek and saw dozens of burrows, most of which were disused. Nicholson recalled the location of every ridge and summit. He could point out most of the species of trees and shrubs, identified numerous birds and guided me flawlessly along overgrown tracks that few people would know about today.

A few hours later the burning sun had disappeared and a big moon rose above Timbertop from the direction of Mount Buller. We spent until midnight spotlighting and came across large numbers of greater gliders. With our torches we explored crystal-clear pools in the creek filled with brown trout. We didn't see any wombats.

In the morning over breakfast Peter declared that we

should climb to the summit of Mount Timbertop. He promised that it would be worth our while and so, just as the sun was beginning to bite at the start of another hot day, we began our ascent. Much of the slope is scree and difficult to clamber up. We were soon sweating and out of breath. The wet forest eventually gave way to an open moss field and then, after another fifty metres, we were on the flat summit, with its ancient forest of gnarled snow gums. From here we could see the huge slab of wilderness where Peter had done his wombatting. He went off by himself for a quiet moment during which he stared across the mountains. I sat under a snow gum, its trunk as hard and cold as steel, and enjoyed this moment on the peak, with this man who had once written a paper about wombats.

I remembered a boyhood occasion when I tried to catch a fish I could see from a bridge. I must have been using the wrong bait—no matter how enticingly I jiggled the juicy prawn, the fish refused to bite. Wombats, I realised on top of Mount Timbertop, left me with the same feeling of frustration. I had looked into their eyes, rubbed their coats, watched them play and talked about them into the night with scientists, yet they remained inaccessible and mysterious to me. In their invisible homes underground, moving to their different beat, they seem highly selective about what is of interest to them—tunnel-visioned. Whatever we may learn about wombats they will never really be interested in us.

We both got up to leave our eyrie on the summit. Nicholson noted our visit in the hikers' logbook kept there: '9 March 2001, P. J. Nicholson 1960. I think the mountain has grown.'

'The mountain has grown,' I replied, 'and the burrows have shrunk.'

We laughed and began the descent.

Bibliography

BOOKS

Aplin, Ken & Archer, Michael, 'Recent Advances in Marsupial Systemics with a New Syncretic Classification' in *Possums and Opossums: Studies in Evolution*, Michael Archer ed., Surrey Beatty & Sons & the Royal Zoological Society of New South Wales, Sydney, 1987.

Archer, Michael, Hand, Suzanne & Godthelp, Henk, *Riversleigh: The Story of Animals in Ancient Rainforests of Inland Australia*, Reed Books, Sydney, 1991.

Australian Dictionary of Biography vol. 2, 1788–1850, I–Z, Melbourne University Press, Melbourne, 1967.

Bass Strait: Australia's Last Frontier, Stephen Murray-Smith ed., ABC Enterprises, Sydney, 1987.

Bondeson, Jan, *Buried Alive: The Terrifying History of Our Most Primal Fear*, W. W. Norton & Co., New York, 2001.

Cayley, Neville, *What Mammal Is That*, Angus & Robertson, Sydney, 1987.

Collins, David, *An Account of the English Colony in New South Wales*, T. Cadell & W. Davies, London, 1802.

Corbett, Laurie, *The Dingo*, Cornell University Press, New York, 1995.

Cuvier, Georges, *Le Règne Animal vol. 2, Les Mammifères*, Fortin, Masson, Paris, 1836–49.

Encyclopedia of Australian Wildlife, Reader's Digest, Sydney, 1997.

Finney, Colin, *To Sail beyond the Sunset*, Rigby, Sydney, 1984.

Flinders, Matthew, *Terra Australis: Great Adventures in the Circumnavigation of Australia*, Tim Flannery ed., Text

Publishing, Melbourne, 2000.

Fortey, Richard, *Life: An Unauthorised Biography, a Natural History of the First Four Thousand Million Years of Life on Earth*, HarperCollins, London, 1997.

Fortey, Richard, *Trilobite*, HarperCollins, London, 2000.

Hill, Robert, *History of the Australian Vegetation: Cretaceous to Recent*, Cambridge University Press, Cambridge, 1994.

Martin, Roger & Handasyde, Katherine, *The Koala*, University of New South Wales Press, Sydney, 1999.

Massola, Aldo, *Bunjil's Cave: Myths, Legends and Superstitions of the Aborigines of South-East Australia*, Lansdowne Press, Melbourne, 1968.

Morris, Jill & Dye, Sharon, *The Wombat Who Talked to the Stars*, Greater Glider Productions, Maleny, Queensland, 1997.

Mulham, William, *'The Best Crossing Place'*, Extracts of the Deniliquin Times, Reliance Printing and Publishing, Deniliquin, 1994.

Nash, Michael, *Cargo for the Colony*, Barxus Press, Sydney, 1996.

Péron, Francois, *Voyage de Découvertes aux Terres Australes...*, Imprimerie Impèriale, Paris, 1807–16.

Persse, Michael, *Well-Ordered Liberty: A Portrait of Geelong Grammar School 1855–1995*, Cliffe Books, Melbourne, 1995.

Ransom, Rosemary, *Taraba: Tasmanian Aboriginal Stories*, DECCD, Tasmania, 1997.

Reed, Alexander, *Myths and Legends of Australia*, Reed Books, Sydney, 1976.

Shaw, George, *General Zoology vol. 1, part 2, 'Quadrupeds'*, S. Kearsley, London, 1800.

Stanbury, Peter & Phipps, Graeme, *Australia's Animals Discovered*, Pergamon Press, Sydney, 1980.

Strahan, Ronald, *Dictionary of Australian Mammal Names*, Angus & Robertson, Sydney, 1981.

Torr, Geordie, *Pythons of Australia*, University of New South Wales Press, Sydney, 2000.

Triggs, Barbara, *The Wombat: Common Wombats in Australia*, University of New South Wales Press, Sydney, 1996.

Troughton, Ellis, *Furred Animals of Australia*, Angus & Robertson, Sydney, 1941.

Watson, Francis, *The Year of the Wombat: England 1857*, Readers Union Group of Book Clubs, Newton Abbot, Devon, 1975.

Wells, Rod, 'Vombatidae' in *Fauna of Australia vol. 1b*, D. A. Walton & B. J. Richardson eds, AGPS, Canberra, 1989.

Wells, Rod & Pridmore, Peter, *Wombats*, Surrey Beatty & Sons, Sydney, 1998.

Winton, Tim, *Blueback*, Pan, Sydney, 1997.

Whitley, Gilbert, *Early History of Australian Zoology*, Royal Zoological Society of New South Wales, Sydney, 1970.

HISTORICAL PAPERS

Anon., 'Observations on Australian Animals', date unknown, State Library of New South Wales, series 35.44.

Joseph Banks collection: extracts of letters from John Hunter to Mr Chalmers, 12 March 1798; from James Thompson to John Schank, 12 September 1798; from Henry Waterhouse to Philip Gidley King, 13 September 1798; from J. Townson to Joseph Banks, 7 May 1798, State Library of New South Wales, series 35.17.

Bass, George, 'Some Account of the Quadruped called Wombat, in New South Wales', date unknown, State Library of New South Wales, series 35.43.

Bass, George, letter to Sir Joseph Banks, 27 May 1799, State Library of New South Wales, series 72.005.

Collins, David, letter to Sir Joseph Banks, 20 July 1804, State Library of New South Wales, series 23.16.

Hunter, John, letter to Sir Joseph Banks, 5 August 1798, State Library of New South Wales, series 38.10.

Hunter, John, copy of a letter to the Literary and Philosophical Society, Newcastle-upon-Tyne, England, 5 August 1798, State Library of New South Wales, series 38.11.

Peers, Louis, letter to Sir Frederick M'Coy, Aratula, 1871.

Price, John, journal extract 'Journey into the Interior of the Country New South Wales', 24 January–2 February 1798, 9 March–2 April 1798, State Library of New South Wales, series 38.21.

JOURNALS

Archer, Michael et al, 'The Evolutionary History and Diversity of Australian Mammals', *Australian Mammalogy* vol. 21, 1999.

Cooper, Des, 'Road Kills of Animals on Some New South Wales Roads', report on data collected by WIRES volunteers in 1997, Macquarie University, Sydney, 1998.

George, H. et al, 'Common Wombats: Rescue, Rehabilitation, Release', Wildlife Information Rescue Service, Sydney, 1995.

Horsup, Alan, 'Recovery Plan for the Northern Hairy-nosed

Wombat', State of Queensland Environment Protection Agency, Brisbane, 1999.

Taylor, Andrea et al, 'Assessing the Consequences of Inbreeding for Population Fitness: Past Challenges and Future Prospects', *Proceedings of the Symposium on Reproduction and Integrated Conservation Science*, Zoological Society of London, 2001.

Taylor, Andrea et al, 'Genetic Variation of Microsatellite Loci in a Bottlenecked Species: the Northern Hairy-nosed Wombat', *Molecular Ecology* vol. 3, 1994.

NEWSPAPERS AND MAGAZINES

Archer, Michael, 'Rossetti and the Wombat', *Apollo*, March 1965.

Bita, Natashia & Cribb, Julian, 'Scientists Target Feral Pest Fertility', *Australian*, 1 November 1995.

'California Trails: Blazing the Way West', *National Geographic* vol. 198, September 2000.

'Common Wombat', Tasmania Parks & Wildlife Service brochure.

George, Helen et al, 'Common Wombats: Rescue, Rehabilitation, Release', Wildlife Information Rescue Service, Sydney, 1995.

Hannan, Liz, 'I Hid in Hole to Escape Attackers', *Sun Herald*, 23 August 1998.

Nicholson, Peter John, 'Wombats', *Timbertop Magazine* no. 8, Geelong Grammar, 1963.

'Queensland Government on the Wombat Trail', *Australian Associated Press*, 14 August 2000.

Reardon, Mitch, 'Secret World of the Wombat', *Australian Geographic*, vol. 30, April–June 1993.

Shimmin, Glenn et al, 'Wombats: How Can They Afford Their High Cost of Housing', *Nature Australia*, Winter 2001.

'Tasmanian Devil and Quoll', Tasmania Parks & Wildlife Service brochure.

Timbertop Magazine no. 6, Geelong Grammar, 1961.

Wroe, Stephen, 'Move over Sabre-tooth Tiger', *Nature Australia*, Spring 2000.

Acknowledgments

My family had to tolerate an enormous amount of inconvenience during the research for this book. Prue was guide, editor, adviser, driver and road-trip co-ordinator. We undertook several major journeys through a number of states and without her the experience would not have been half as much fun. Sophie has spent the first ten months of her life in a world where her father was obsessed with wombats and as a result has endured too much time in her car seat. My sons Angus and Finn have been unfailingly supportive, and I am more grateful for their interest than they now realise. Their love of wild things is a joy to watch.

Stuart Cohen inspired me to concentrate on this wombat book at a time when I was casting around for my next writing project. He also provided introductions and information. My publisher Michael Heyward has once again humbled me with his capacity to understand a project. I also thank Melanie Ostell for her editing suggestions and Text's other staff, all of whom fielded my countless calls. Fiona Inglis, my agent, provided an immense amount of support and encouragement.

I owe special thanks to Rod Wells and Barbara Triggs. Wells gave me numerous anecdotes and told me of Rossetti's love affair with wombats. Day after day both he and Barbara Triggs took calls about wombat biology and it was Triggs who directed me towards Narawntapu National Park. I have relied heavily on their seminal texts, full of fascinating wombat facts. I recommend them to readers of this book.

Faye and David Garnock introduced me to baby wombats and are an inspiration. I wish to thank Nick Mooney and Geoff King in Tasmania, both of whom found me a place to sleep and gave me large slabs of their time. The staff at Timbertop were enormously helpful as was Michael Collins Persse from Geelong Grammar; the Anderson family gave me a place to stay near Timbertop.

Thanks to the staff of both Taronga and Western Plains zoos—especially Darill Clements, David Blyde and Mark Williams. Philip Maher and Stephen Seymour were kind enough to take me to the Deniliquin burrows, and Martin Driver also helped. Alan Horsup was generous in sharing his knowledge; I also thank him for the efforts he made to show me a northern hairy-nosed wombat.

Peter Temple-Smith gave me information and put me in contact with Ron Dibben, who also was unfailingly helpful. Gaylene and Rob Parker tolerated my intrusion into their busy schedule, feeding orphaned wombats.

In respect to the historical material I thank Paul Brunton, Samantha Fenton, Sandy Ingleby, Carol Cantrell and David Pemberton. Tim Smith from the NSW Heritage Office helped with the *Sydney Cove* facts.

Heidi de Wald of the Australian Museum was instrumental in organising the Riversleigh trip. Henk Godthelp, Phil Creaser and Mike Archer also made that visit possible. Andrea Taylor introduced me to wombat genetics and helped me to understand it.

Without the assistance, advice and patience of Peter Nicholson this book would certainly not have been possible.

Index